EDGE OF ARMAGEDDON

Florida and the Cuban Missile Crisis

NICK WYNNE AND
JOE KNETSCH, EDITORS

outskirts
press

Table of Contents

Documents

WASHINGTON, *October 22, 1962*

Good evening my fellow citizens:

This Government, as promised, has maintained the closest surveillance of the Soviet military buildup on the island of Cuba. Within the past week, unmistakable evidence has established the fact that a series of offensive missile sites is now in preparation on that imprisoned island. The purpose of these bases can be none other than to provide a nuclear strike capability against the Western Hemisphere.

Upon receiving the first preliminary hard information of this nature last Tuesday morning at 9A.M., I directed that our surveillance be stepped up. And having now confirmed and completed our evaluation of the evidence and our decision on a course of action, this Government feels obliged to report this new crisis to you in fullest detail.

The characteristics of these new missile sites indicate two distinct types of installations. Several of them include medium range ballistic missiles, capable of carrying a nuclear warhead for a distance of more than 1,000 nautical miles. Each of these missiles, in short, is capable of striking Washington, D. C., the Panama Canal, Cape Canaveral, Mexico City, or any other city in the southeastern part of the United States, in Central America, or in the Caribbean area.

Additional sites not yet completed appear to be designed for intermediate range ballistic missiles—capable of traveling more than twice as far—and thus capable of striking most of the major cities in the Western Hemisphere, ranging as far north as Hudson Bay, Canada, and as far south as Lima, Peru. In addition, jet bombers, capable of carrying nuclear weapons, are now being uncrated and assembled in Cuba, while the necessary air bases are being prepared.

This urgent transformation of Cuba into an important strategic base—by the presence of these large, long-range, and clearly offensive weapons of sudden mass destruction--constitutes an explicit threat to the peace and security of all the Americas, in flagrant and deliberate defiance of the Rio Pact of 1947, the traditions of this Nation and hemisphere, the joint resolution of the 87th Congress, the Charter of the United Nations, and my own public warnings to the Soviets on September 4 and 13. This action also contradicts the repeated assurances of Soviet spokesmen, both publicly and privately delivered, that the arms buildup in Cuba would retain its original defensive character, and that the Soviet Union had no need or desire to station strategic missiles. on the territory of any other nation.

The size of this undertaking makes clear that it has been planned for some months. Yet only last month, after I had made clear the distinction between any introduction of ground-to-ground missiles and the existence of defensive antiaircraft missiles, the Soviet Government publicly stated on September 11 that, and I quote, "the armaments and military equipment sent to Cuba are designed exclusively for defensive purposes," that, and I quote the Soviet Government, "there is no need for the Soviet Government to shift its weapons .. for a retaliatory blow to any other country, for instance Cuba," and that, and I quote their government, "the Soviet Union has so powerful rockets to carry these nuclear warheads that there is no need to search for sites for them beyond the boundaries of the Soviet Union." That statement was false.

Only last Thursday, as evidence of this rapid offensive buildup was already in my hand, Soviet Foreign Minister Gromyko told me in my office that he was instructed to make it clear once again, as he said his government had already done, that Soviet assistance to Cuba, and I quote, "pursued solely the purpose of contributing to the defense capabilities of Cuba," that, and I quote him, "training by Soviet specialists of Cuban nationals in handling defensive armaments was by no means offensive, and if it were otherwise," Mr. Gromyko went on, "the Soviet Government would never become involved in rendering such assistance." That statement also was false.

Neither the United States of America nor the world community of nations can tolerate deliberate deception and offensive threats on the part of any nation, large or small. We no longer live in a world where only the actual firing of weapons represents a sufficient challenge to a nation's security to constitute maximum peril. Nuclear weapons are so destructive and ballistic missiles are so swift, that any substantially increased possibility of their use or any sudden change in their deployment may well be regarded as a definite threat to peace.

For many years, both the Soviet Union and the United States, recognizing this fact, have deployed strategic nuclear weapons with great care, never upsetting the precarious status quo which insured that these weapons would not be used in the absence of some vital challenge. Our own strategic missiles have never been transferred to the territory of any other nation under a cloak of secrecy and deception; and our history—unlike that of the Soviets since the end of World War II-- demonstrates that we have no desire to dominate or conquer any other nation or impose our system upon its people. Nevertheless, American citizens have become adjusted to living daily on the bull's-eye of Soviet missiles located inside the U.S.S.R. or in submarines.

In that sense, missiles in Cuba add to an already clear and present danger—although it should be noted the nations of Latin America have never previously been subjected to a potential nuclear threat.

But this secret, swift, and extraordinary buildup of Communist missiles—in an area well known to have a special and historical relationship to the United States and the nations of the Western Hemisphere, in violation of Soviet assurances, and in defiance of American and hemispheric policy—this sudden, clandestine decision to station strategic weapons for the first time outside of Soviet soil—is a deliberately provocative and unjustified change in the status quo which cannot be accepted by this country, if our courage and our commitments are ever to be trusted again by either friend or foe.

The 1930's taught us a clear lesson: aggressive conduct, if allowed to go unchecked, ultimately leads to war. This nation is opposed to war. We are also true to our word. Our unswerving objective, therefore, must be to prevent the use of these missiles against this or any other country, and to secure their withdrawal or elimination from the Western Hemisphere.

Our policy has been one of patience and restraint, as befits a peaceful and powerful nation, which leads a worldwide alliance. We have been determined not to be diverted from our central concerns by mere irritants and fanatics. But now further action is required-and it is under way; and these actions may only be the beginning. We will not prematurely or unnecessarily risk the costs of worldwide nuclear war in which even the fruits of victory would be ashes in our mouth-but neither will we shrink from that risk at any time it must be faced.

Acting, therefore, in the defense of our own security and of the entire Western Hemisphere, and under the authority entrusted to me by the Constitution as endorsed by the Resolution of the Congress, I have directed that the following *initial* steps be taken immediately:

First: To halt this offensive buildup, a strict quarantine on all offensive military equipment under shipment to Cuba is being initiated. All ships of any kind bound for Cuba from whatever nation or port will, if found to contain cargoes of offensive weapons, be turned back. This quarantine will be extended, if needed, to other types of cargo and carriers. We are not at this time, however, denying the necessities of life as the Soviets attempted to do in their Berlin blockade of 1948.

Second: I have directed the continued and increased close surveillance of Cuba and its military buildup. The foreign ministers of the OAS, In their communiqué' of October 6, rejected secrecy on such matters in this hemisphere. Should these offensive military preparations continue, thus increasing the threat to the hemisphere, further action will be justified. I have directed the Armed Forces to prepare for any eventualities; and I trust that in the interest of both the Cuban people and the Soviet technicians at the sites, the hazards to all concerned of continuing this threat will be recognized.

Third: It shall be the policy of this Nation to regard any nuclear missile launched from Cuba against any nation in the Western Hemisphere as an attack by the Soviet Union on the United States, requiring a full retaliatory response upon the Soviet Union.

Fourth: As a necessary military precaution, I have reinforced our base at Guantanamo, evacuated today the dependents of our personnel there, and ordered additional military units to be on a standby alert basis.

Fifth: We are calling tonight for an immediate meeting of the Organ of Consultation under the Organization of American States, to consider this threat to hemispheric security and to invoke articles 6 and 8 of the Rio Treaty in support of all necessary action. The United Nations Charter allows for regional security arrangements-and the nations of this hemisphere decided long ago against the military presence of outside powers. Our other allies around the world have also been alerted.

Sixth: Under the Charter of the United Nations, we are asking tonight that an emergency meeting of the Security Council be convoked without delay to take action against this latest Soviet threat to world peace. Our resolution will call for the prompt dismantling and withdrawal of all offensive weapons in Cuba, under the supervision of U.N. observers, before the quarantine can be lifted.

Seventh and finally: I call upon Chairman Khrushchev to halt and eliminate this clandestine, reckless, and provocative threat to world peace and to stable relations between our two nations. I call upon him further to abandon this course of world domination, and to join in an historic effort to end the perilous arms race and to transform the history of man. He has an opportunity now to move the world back from the abyss of destruction-by returning to his government's own words that it had no need to station missiles outside its own territory, and withdrawing these weapons from Cuba-by refraining from any action which will widen or deepen the present crisis-and then by participating in a search for peaceful and permanent solutions.

This Nation is prepared to present its case against the Soviet threat to peace, and our own proposals for a peaceful world, at any time and in any forum-in the OAS, in the United Nations, or in any other meeting that could be useful-without limiting our freedom of action. We have in the past made strenuous efforts to limit the spread of nuclear weapons. We have proposed the elimination of all arms and military bases in a fair and effective disarmament treaty. We are prepared to discuss new proposals for the removal of tensions on both sides—including the possibilities of a genuinely independent Cuba, free to determine its own destiny. We have no wish to war with the Soviet Union—for we are a peaceful people who desire to live in peace with all other peoples.

But it is difficult to settle or even discuss these problems in an atmosphere of intimidation. That is why this latest Soviet threat—or any other threat which is made either independently or in response to our actions this week—must and will be met with determination. Any hostile move anywhere in the world against the safety and freedom of peoples to whom we are committed—including in particular the brave people of West Berlin—will be met by whatever action is needed.

Finally, I want to say a few words to the captive people of Cuba, to whom this speech is being directly carried by special radio facilities. I speak to you as a friend, as one who knows of your deep attachment to your fatherland, as one who shares your aspirations for liberty and justice for all. And I have watched and the American people have watched with deep sorrow how your nationalist revolution was betrayed-and how your fatherland fell under foreign domination. Now your leaders are no longer Cuban leaders inspired by Cuban ideals. They are puppets and agents of an international conspiracy which has turned Cuba against your friends and neighbors in the Americas-and turned it into the first Latin American country to become a target for nuclear war—the first Latin American country to have these weapons on its soil.

These new weapons are not in your interest. They contribute nothing to your peace and well-being. They can only undermine it. But this country has no wish to cause you to suffer or to impose any system upon you. We know that your lives and land are being used as pawns by those who deny your freedom. Many times in the past, the Cuban people have risen to throw out tyrants who destroyed their liberty. And I have no doubt that most Cubans today look forward to the time when they will be truly free-free from foreign domination, free to choose their own leaders, free to select their own system, free to own their own land, free to speak and write and worship without fear or degradation. And then shall Cuba be welcomed back to the society of free nations and to the associations of this hemisphere.

My fellow citizens: let no one doubt that this is a difficult and dangerous effort on which we have set out. No one can foresee precisely what course it will take or what costs or casualties will be incurred. Many months of sacrifice and self-discipline lie ahead—months in which both our patience and our will will be tested—months in which many threats and denunciations will keep us aware of our dangers. But the greatest danger of all would be to do nothing.

The path we have chosen for the present is full of hazards, as all paths are—but it is the one most consistent with our character and courage as a nation and our commitments around the world. The cost of freedom is always high-but Americans have always paid it. And one path we shall never choose, and that is the path of surrender or submission.

Our goal is not the victory of might, but the vindication of right-not peace at the expense of freedom, but both peace *and* freedom, here in this hemisphere, and, we hope, around the world. God willing, that goal will be achieved.

Thank you and good night.

Speech to the American People by President John F. Kennedy, October 22, 1962

BY THE PRESIDENT OF THE UNITED STATES OF AMERICA
A PROCLAMATION

WHEREAS the peace of the world and the security of the United States and of all American states are endangered by reason of the establishment by the Sino-Soviet powers of an offensive military capability in Cuba, including bases for ballistic missiles with a potential range covering most of North and South America;

WHEREAS by a joint resolution passed by the Congress of the United States and approved on October 3, 1962, it was declared that the United States is determined to prevent by whatever means may be necessary, including the use of arms, the Marxist-Leninist regime in Cuba from expanding, by force or the threat of force, its aggressive or subversive activities to any part of this hemisphere, and to prevent in Cuba the creation or use of an externally supported military capability endangering the security of the United States; and

WHEREAS the Organ of Consultation of the American Republics meeting in Washington on October 23, 1962, recommended that the member states, in accordance with Articles 6 and 8 of the Inter-American Treaty of Reciprocal Assistance, take all measures, individually and collectively, including the use of armed force, which they may deem necessary to insure that the Government of Cuba cannot continue to receive from the Sino-Soviet powers military material and related supplies which may threaten the peace and security of the continent and to prevent the missiles in Cuba with offensive capability from ever becoming an active threat to the peace and security of the continents:

Now, THEREFORE, I, John F. Kennedy, President of the United States of America, acting under and by virtue of the authority conferred upon me by the Constitution and statutes of the United States, in accordance with the aforementioned resolutions of the United States Congress and of the Organ of Consultation of the American Republics, and to defend the security of the United States, do hereby proclaim that the forces under my command are ordered, beginning at 2:00 P.M. Greenwich time October 24, 1962, to interdict, subject to the instructions herein contained, the delivery of offensive weapons and associated material to Cuba.

For the purposes of this proclamation, the following are declared to be prohibited material:

Surface-to-surface missiles; bomber aircraft; bombs; air-to-surface rockets and guided missiles; warheads for any of the above weapons; mechanical or electronic equipment to support or operate the above items; and any other classes of material hereafter designated by the Secretary of Defense for the purpose of effectuating this proclamation.

To enforce this order, the Secretary of Defense shall take appropriate measures to prevent the delivery of prohibited material to Cuba, employing the land, sea and air forces of the United States in cooperation with any forces that may be made available by other American states.

The Secretary of Defense may make such regulations and issue such directives as he deems necessary to ensure the effectiveness of this order, including the designation, within a reasonable distance of Cuba, of prohibited or restricted zones and of prescribed routes.

Any vessel or craft which may be proceeding toward Cuba may be intercepted and may be directed to identify itself, its cargo, equipment, and stores and its ports of call, to stop, to lie to, to submit to visit and search, or to proceed as directed. Any vessel or craft which fails or refuses to respond to or comply with directions shall be subjected to being taken into custody. Any vessel or craft which is believed en route to Cuba and may be carrying prohibited material or may itself constitute such material shall, wherever possible, be directed to proceed to another destination of its own choice and shall be taken into custody if it fails or refuses to obey such directions. All vessels or craft taken into custody shall be sent into a port of the United States for appropriate disposition.

In carrying out this order, force shall not be used except in case of failure or refusal to comply with directions, or with regulations or directives of the Secretary of Defense issued hereunder, after reasonable efforts have been made to communicate them to the vessel or craft, or in case of self-defense. k any case, force shall be used only to the extent necessary.

IN WITNESS WHEREOF, I have hereunto set my hand and caused the seal of the United States of America to be affixed.

Done in the city of Washington this 23d day of October in the year of Our Lord, 1962, and of the independence of the United States of America the 187th

JOHN F. KENNEDY
By the President:

Dean Rusk, Secretary of State

Preface

The impact of the Cuban Missile on the state of Florida was tremendous. The state saw the immediate influx of over 100,000 troops, a large number of air-wings being transferred to Florida bases and the attention of the entire population of the state was focused upon the events unfolding in front of them. The tension of those October days filled the air as the nation and the world faced the prospect of nuclear war. No state felt this tension more than Florida. Changes in school curriculum, Civil Defense procedures and governmental relations took place almost overnight. No one escaped the feeling of those frightening days.

But not everyone experienced the same feelings and changes in the same way. Orlando, for example, saw the relative calm of McCoy AFB change quickly with the arrival of the U-2 group. The pace definitely quickened in and around Homestead AFB with the transfer of nearly 10,000 troops to the defense of the base and possible inclusion in the proposed invasion force and the stationing of new fighter wings to protect the area from possible attack. Opa Locka became the headquarters for all CIA interrogations of Cuban nationals bringing information as to Soviet troop and missile movements within Cuba. Governor Farris Bryant became the national leader in Civil Defense preparations and educational changes to meet the Soviet challenge. Pensacola Naval Air Station became extremely active in coastal patrols and being on alert for assistance needed to protect the ships maintaining the "quarantine" of Cuba. Indeed, every defense facility in the state was affected by the crisis and the potential for war.

Civilian response was also very quick and intense. Air raid shelters became the *cause dejour* for homeowners and businesses. Some larger fall out facilities were constructed in places like Fort Clinch State Park, city halls and other public buildings. Schools, auditoriums and other large buildings were examined for their potential use in protecting the public from possible radiation fall out from atomic weapons, if they were used. Florida had the additional worry, especially in the southern portion of the state, from fall out due to potential bombing of Cuba by American forces. Shipping rations to these shelters became a major concern of all transportation authorities, be they the State Road Department or the railroads. Civilian flights were limited and a high state of alert kept everyone on edge. It was a very difficult time for all.

The purpose of this volume is to document and reflect upon the Florida experience during the Cuban Missile Crisis. It was unique and had an impact on all Floridians. The focus is upon the local responses and memories within the larger picture of the national effort. To date, the focus has been upon the policies of the Kennedy administration, the diplomatic difficulties and the sense of doom generated by the crisis. Few states, especially Florida, have had their records, local and state, explored and explained relative to the international situation created by the crisis. Our goal is to fill in the gap for Florida and encourage others to follow through with more detailed research, writing and analysis.

Local press coverage was somewhat restricted because of the possibility of war, but the tremendous disruption of local activities and the public presence of troop camps, missile batteries, countless convoys of troops and materiel, and over flights of aircraft created speculation and led to extended conversations. Given the brevity of the crisis and the lack of fulltime news coverage, the limited number of photographs available to scholars is limited, and, like the nation's political and military leaders, researchers are forced to rely on the grainy, sometimes fuzzy, pictures captured by fast moving and highflying reconnaissance aircraft. In this volume, we are very much interested in the impact the crisis, though short, had on local populations.

Nick Wynne
Joe Knetsch

Contributors

Nick Wynne is the Executive Director Emeritus of the Florida Historical Society and the author/co-author/editor of approximately twenty-seven historical books and novels. He has published frequently.

Joe Knetsch retired from the Florida Department of Natural Resources and is currently working as a consultant for several legal firms, private individuals, and government agencies. A prolific researcher and author, he has published extensively.

Janet DeVries Naughton, a Lantana resident, is an Associate Professor, Librarian at Palm Beach State College. She holds a master's degree in Library and Information Science from Florida State University, and a baccalaureate degree in history from Florida Atlantic University where she is completing a master's degree in history. She is the past president of the Boynton Beach Historical Society, author, co-author or editor of eight local history books and moonlights as a tour guide in a historic Florida cemetery.

James A. Schnur is a native of St. Petersburg in Pinellas County, where he taught college-level courses in Florida history for nearly 20 years. He is an expert in archival management, and an authority on Tampa Bay regional history. He is the author of several books.

Robert Redd is one of the rare Floridians who can honestly say he is a native, born and raised in the state. He is a graduate of Stetson University, in DeLand, with a degree in American Studies. He currently serves as the Executive Director for the New Smyrna Museum of History. He also serves as a volunteer on the Volusia County Historic Preservation Board. He is a member of several historical groups and societies including the Southern Historical Association, the Florida Historical Society, the St. Augustine Historical Society, the Civil War Trust, the Southeast Volusia Historical Society, and others.

Joy Wallace Dickinson grew up in Orlando, where she remembers seeing alligators in the lake across from her family's home in Thornton Park. A former editor at the Institute of Early American History in Williamsburg, Va., she has written hundreds of "Florida Flashback" features in the *Orlando Sentinel* about many episodes in Central Florida's past. She's also the author of three books including *Orlando: City of Dreams*. She lives near Lake Eola Park in downtown Orlando.

Dean Debolt is the Special Collections Librarian at the University of West Florida in Pensacola. He is also a respected historian, a diligent researcher, and the author of numerous articles and papers

Introduction

The Kennedy-Nixon debates and the campaign that was shaped in part by them, stressed the importance of Cuba in the American conscience. Kennedy alleged that the United States had fallen behind in the production of nuclear warheads and that our delivery system was lagging behind the Russians, Cuba's now friendly ally. Although the so-called "Missile Gap" did not exist in reality; it was a major concern among American voters and candidates vying for their support. Kennedy had hit upon the "missile gap" and the strengthening regime in Cuba run by Fidel Castro and supporters of the 26th of July Movement as major themes that provoked emotional responses from voters. The Democratic candidate painted the Eisenhower administration with the blame for allowing these things to happen. By tying the "missile gap", the growth of Castroism and national security together, Kennedy hit upon a sore nerve with which to attack his political rival, Richard Nixon, who had been Eisenhower's vice president. It was an effective strategy, and one that helped him to become president at the height of the Cold War.

During the campaign candidate Kennedy posited the idea that the best way to remove Castro would be to train Cuban exiles for an invasion of Cuba to reclaim their country. At the time that he introduced his novel idea, the Eisenhower administration had already begun just such a program under control of the Central Intelligence Agency (CIA). Castro became somewhat of a fixation of President Kennedy throughout his administration. Kennedy had chided his political rivals for not getting rid of the Cuban dictator and set it up as a goal of his tenure to do just that. His administration, still new and naïve in foreign policy matters, almost immediately backed various attempts on Castro's life and encouraged exile raids into Cuba to destroy crops, upset industry and cripple communications. Aside from adding additional destruction to an already weak economy, the major impacts of these acts were to drive Castro's government into further suppression of human rights, to strengthen the fears of Cubans loyal to Castro of a possible invasion by the United States, and to force Castro to look further abroad for economic and military support. The only country which could supply Castro with his immediate needs was the Soviet Union, which was eager to establish a close relationship with a country so close to the United States and which was amenable to exporting revolution into Latin America, even if that country was not following the Soviet model.

Castro's rule threatened the United States, as "Cold Warrior" Kennedy perceived it, in a number of ways. The spread of communist ideology throughout Latin America and the undermining of the United States political leadership in the Western Hemisphere, Kennedy thought, was the biggest threat of an enduring Castro regime. Castro's alliance with the Soviet Union also represented a nullification of the sacred Monroe Doctrine which allegedly denied any European expansion into the Western Hemisphere; which Castro's agreements with the Soviets appeared to violate openly. The flaunting of the Monroe Doctrine was seen as a defiance of American interests and leadership in Latin America and the Caribbean. The possibility that the Soviets might set up a puppet state in Cuba and threaten the security of the United States by sending troops, military equipment and technological assistance was never far from American minds. During the presidential campaign, Kennedy had strongly implied he would take an active role in Cuba and frequently mentioned the removal of Castro. Both his supporters and the Republican opposition anxiously waited to see what the new president would do. The pressure was on the new administration to do something positive about getting Castro out of the way.

Kennedy's administration also brought in a new defense doctrine put forth by the new head of the Joint Chiefs of Staff, Maxwell Taylor. General Taylor had formulated a new military policy toward the end of the Eisenhower administration and referred to it as "Flexible Response." This policy emphasized a military establishment that would meet every new challenge with troops, transportation, and rapid response. This contrasted sharply with the Eisenhower administration's "massive retaliation" policy which relied upon the United States' nuclear advantage in power and number of warheads and delivery systems. The Eisenhower administration saw this as a more economical defense posture, requiring far fewer troops and equipment. It relied upon nuclear superiority as a deterrence factor while building up local abilities to resist insurgency and revolution. General Taylor believed there was a "need for a capability to react across the entire spectrum of possible challenge, for coping with anything from general atomic war to infiltrations." Just as important, he also noted, "it is just as necessary to deter or win quickly limited wars as to deter general wars." The United States needed, he strongly believed, a quick response to dangers that would help the United States avoid piecemeal attrition by becoming involved in many small wars which had the potential to grow into general wars involving the nuclear powers. Massive retaliation should be scrapped as the national defense policy before something triggered it by accident. He had the backing, for the most part, of the new Secretary of Defense, Robert McNamara. The Secretary, while agreeing with much of Taylor's analysis, still insisted upon a system that ensured survival and the ability to launch the second or third retaliatory nuclear strike without difficulty. For this to happen, the administration needed to develop a highly effective command and control system that was economical at the same time. General Taylor stuck by his guns and noted that nuclear weapons had produced a state of mutual deterrence which translated to a near stalemate in time of war. Future wars, Taylor strongly argued, would be of a limited nature with a need to commit ground forces in some areas. The costs of both forms of defense advocated by Taylor and McNamara would be high, and budget fights would be long and difficult unless the economy picked up beyond what was forecast at the time. It was a challenge that would be difficult to overcome, even with Democratic control of both houses.

With a new philosophy of defense, political pressure from both sides of the congressional aisle, and a need for action to demonstrate his administrations "can do" determination, Kennedy was brought into the orbit of the Eisenhower concept of removing Castro via the use of Cuban exiles, trained by the CIA. The plan had been hatched by the "Special Group" in early 1960 (this group was a part of the National Security Council which approved covert actions). By April of that year, the CIA, as instructed by the Special Group, had formulated a plan of action which would emphasize propaganda, the creation of a unified Cuban opposition to Castro, and would revolve around a cadre of about twenty Cuban exiles, trained in guerilla tactics of infiltration, sabotage and communications. This group was to recruit and train a hundred or more exiles who would then be placed in Cuba to infiltrate various groups or raise forces against Castro in the Escambray Mountains. This would be a very difficult task for even the best organized and funded intelligence services, according to former CIA Director, Richard Helms. The output from this group became known as Operation Zapata, modeled on the CIA's overthrow of the Jacobo Arbenz government in Guatemala in 1954. The final number of trained men to carry out the infiltration of Cuba and begin the new revolution to oust Castro was approximately 1,400 men. It was almost impossible to keep a covert operation of this magnitude secret and it was not long before Castro's intelligence service knew almost every detail of Operation Zapata. By the time the planned invasion took place, Castro had his air force, a 25,000-man army and the nation's reserve militia of over 200,000 on alert for the arrival of the exiles. The result was a foregone conclusion.

Much has been written about the Bay of Pigs fiasco but its greatest impact may have been on President Kennedy who never forgot the bungling affair. The Director of the CIA at the time was long-time intelligence man, Allen Dulles, the brother of Secretary of State, John Foster Dulles. His assistant in this affair was also a well-seasoned veteran of foreign affairs and intelligence, Richard Bissell. The planning for Operation Zapata lacked certain fundamentals, such as not knowing the geography of the area and not realizing that the swampy area of the Bay of Pigs was much less desirable than the original site at Trinidad, which was drier and closer to the Escambray Mountains. Counterintelligence activities were left to only one operative, who try as he might, could not support an operation of 1,400 men effectively. Infiltration by Castro's agents was important as was maintaining a constant watch on the training areas near Miami and in Guatemala. There were constant miscommunications between the CIA planners and the administration in Washington, which seemed somewhat ambivalent about the operation. Kennedy and his associates had grave misgivings concerning the invasion, but did not think they could halt the operation before it went off. Of the twenty or so advisors that Kennedy consulted, only Senator J. William Fulbright opposed the plan. The Joint Chiefs of Staff were not directly consulted and only reviewed the plan and would not commit themselves to it nor offer any constructive criticism, seemingly saying, "it's the CIA's game." Dulles and Bissell assumed that the new Kennedy administration would allow the invasion to receive air cover if it became obvious that the invasion was in trouble. After all, Eisenhower had allowed air support to come to the aid of rebels during the Guatemalan invasion. The anticipated air cover was not forthcoming, and the men on the beaches of the Bay of Pigs took a beating, which left 114 dead and 1,189 captured. In the aftermath of the failed invasion, both Dulles and Bissell insisted that they never had told the president that there would be an immediate uprising of the Cuban populace that would bring down Castro, which had been assumed by most officials in the administration. Kennedy, who had no background in these kind of operations, wanted deniability and a quiet landing of the invasion force. Neither of his desires were possible, and the latter was an absurd expectation. Revolutions need noise and publicity to spread the word and cause mass defections of the population, and Kennedy's desires were unrealistic. There were many other problems with this operation and its failure had a devastating effect on confidence of Kennedy, who took full responsibility for the event.

Kennedy may have been chastised, but he was not finished trying to remove Castro or destroying his Communist regime. The next big project was Operation Mongoose, headed by General Edward Lansdale, whose expertise was counterintelligence. Most of the thirty-three different schemes associated with this operation were targeted against the economy of Cuba, although some assassination attempts on Castro were also part of the operation. In an interview General Fabian Escalante, former head of Castro's security, told Gaeton Fonzi in 1996 that there were at least 142 attempts on Castro's life during the first years after the Bay of Pigs, which the General attributed to U.S. influence or operatives. The concept of the operation was simple: "The political actions will be assisted by economic warfare to induce failure of the Communist regime to supply Cuba's economic needs, psychological operations to turn the people's resentment increasingly against the regime, and military-type groups to give the popular movement an action arm for sabotage and armed resistance in support of political objectives." The plan also boosted the growth of the CIA interrogation center in Opa Locka, Florida from a staff of two to one of thirty-four working fulltime to retrieve the most current information about conditions in Cuba from the newest refugees. The first Lansdale report admitted the failure of the CIA to induce rebellion or to produce the necessary political agents to spark resistance. Although this operation was completely controlled by the CIA, one of the "tasks" enunciated by Lansdale was for the Department of Defense to submit a contingency plan for the use of U. S. military force to support a popular resistance movement, assuming one ever emerged. This report is dated January 18, 1962. A second report, dated July 25, 1962 outlined possible courses of action open to the United States in Cuba. Option one was to simply accept Castro's Cuba as a member of the Soviet bloc and to try and protect the rest of the hemisphere. Option two was to exert all possible pressure—economic, political, psychological and diplomatic—to overthrow the regime without committing U. S. troops or any "overt employment of U. S. Military." The third option was to commit the U. S. to help the Cubans overthrow Castro with a step-by-step phasing in of U. S. forces to ensure success, if required. Finally, the last option was to use "a provocation" and overthrow the Castro regime by U. S. military forces. The only problem with the Lansdale plan was its lack of backing by the Joint Chiefs and the Secretary of Defense. None of the options offered the deniability desired by Kennedy, and the U. S. lacked the ability to send its messages effectively to Cuba via short wave because the Cuban people did not have many of the receivers to hear the signals. In addition, Operation Mongoose faced the likelihood of abject failure because "we have been unable to surface the Cuban resistance potential to a point where we can measure it realistically." In other words, Operation Mongoose, up to this point, had failed to arouse any resistance to Castro in Cuba thereby nullifying any real chance for the U. S. to directly overthrow Castro without making a further muddle of it. Kennedy would not stand for another embarrassment on the order of the Bay of Pigs. Indeed, when a more absurd "Operation Northwoods" was proposed, Secretary McNamara bluntly refused to consider it.

The coming crisis between the United States, Cuba and the Soviet Union did not happen in a vacuum. The negotiations over the outbreak of violence in Laos had just concluded at this point and a supposed agreement had been tentatively reached, but this was just an interlude in an extended civil war that would last until 1975. The problem of

Russian activities in Berlin and the possibility of a Soviet attack was constantly on Kennedy's mind. Negotiations for the creation of the Organization of American States were ongoing and the problem of what to do with Castro's Cuba hotly debated by other American nations. In the end, the United States had its way and Cuba was banned from the organization with some very important countries abstaining from the vote.

A revolt in the Congo drew some attention away from the major problems faced by the U.S. but there was little danger of our becoming involved in that conflict at the time. And, of course, the question of how much aid to send to South Viet Nam was a very involved topic with the concept of Flexible Response being geared towards that hotspot. On top of all the foreign affairs problems, the Civil Rights movement at home, with the admission of James Meredith into the University of Mississippi, presented the Kennedy administration with another major problem. In the turmoil created by numerous foreign and domestic problems facing the new administration, Cuba was relegated to the status of a potential threat that would best be handled by a policy of isolation and watchful waiting.

Just as John F. Kennedy faced numerous problems as a new president, so, too, did the Soviet premier, Nikita Khrushchev, who had assumed the leadership of the Soviet Union in 1958. Josef Stalin, who had ruled the Soviet Union from 1924 until 1953, had concentrated all political, economic, and military power in his hands. Following his death, the Soviet Union went through a period of political instability and multiple leaders before Khrushchev emerged as premier. Promising to reverse the iron-handed policies of control prevalent during the Stalin era, he faced a myriad of problems internally and externally. First, Khrushchev was cognizant that the Russian military and intelligence services had to be placated at all costs in order to preserve his position and to prevent his overthrow. To do this, it was necessary that he present to the world a strong image of the Soviet Union as a major power determined to oppose the United States and its allies in military conflicts and political upheavals around the globe. Second, he faced the problem of improving the position of the Soviet Union and its allies in the "Cold War" power struggle by adding new allies, creating political and military difficulties for the United States, maintaining constant pressure of western nations by employing the threat of nuclear war, and suppressing opposition to Soviet control in its various satellite nations. The Hungarian uprising of 1956, although suppressed, haunted Soviet military and political leaders. Khrushchev also was expected to do something to blunt the effectiveness of the network of military alliances created by the United States and which encircled the Soviet Union and its allies. Finally, Khrushchev was expected to strengthen a Soviet economy that depended largely on military expenditures and which provided little in the way of consumerism. Failure to achieve solutions to these problems would give his opponents an excuse to remove him from power.

Faced with the need to demonstrate his ability to govern effectively, Khrushchev welcomed the change in political leadership in the United States. John Kennedy, unlike his predecessors Harry Truman and Dwight D. Eisenhower, was untested and unproven in the arena of foreign policy and might be easier to manipulate. Although allegedly liking the new president, Khrushchev considered him a "Cold Warrior" type, but easier to work with than his political opponent, Richard Nixon, who had engaged the premier in the famous "Kitchen Debate." Kennedy, at the Vienna Conference in June 1961, felt that Khrushchev had "bullied" him on some issues and came away from that critical conference with the idea that the Soviet leader considered him "weak" and was willing to test him on a number of issues. Kennedy conceded in an interview with the New York Times James Reston, "that Khrushchev 'just beat the hell out of me.' He would now have to prove his mettle." By August 1961, following an American build-up of 150,000 troops, expanding the draft and winning an additional $3.25 billion in his defense budget, Kennedy was prepared to take on the tough talking Khrushchev.

The first confrontation was quick in coming. On August 13, 1961, the Soviet premier ordered his East German ally to string up a barbed wire fence around its section of Berlin, replaced shortly thereafter with a brick wall, and facing down a hostile American move in that city. For Khrushchev, this violation of the World War II agreement of free movement of persons in the old German capital was something the Soviet leader considered a victory. Although facing many problems himself with the East Germans, Khrushchev pointed to the new wall as a Soviet victory in the Cold War and a humiliation for the United States, its allies, and the young president in Washington.

Khrushchev also had to worry about the U. S. surrounding the Soviet Union and its allies in the Warsaw Pact, with nuclear missiles in Italy, Turkey, West Germany and England, all capable of wiping out most Soviet industries, military bases and political targets. Fidel Castro's Cuba offered the Soviets an opportunity to redress this strategic imbalance with the placement of Russian nuclear missiles batteries on the island. Khrushchev would gamble on this gambit, not only to redress the nuclear imbalance, but to strengthen the Soviet Union's presence in Latin America. A successful operation in the Western Hemisphere would satisfy his military opponents at home, offer a deterrent to the use of American missiles that ringed the Soviet Union and its satellites, and solidify the Soviet position as a major world power. He would also be preserving his new communist ally, Cuba, from further invasion by the United States or some other Latin American state allied with it. If he could pull this all off, Khrushchev would strengthen his own position internationally and at home.

Operation "Anadyr" was the result of Khrushchev's reading of the situation in Cuba and information from the local KGB operatives and others. It was an elaborate affair using the best practices of "Maskirovka" (deception) and was headed by Colonel General Semyon Ivanov. Only five officers of the General Staff were involved in the decision-making process, but there was considerable debate among other civilian and military advisers as to how this could be achieved without the secret leaking out. Security for the operation was so strict that no secretaries were used to type the proposals, and everything was hand-written and hand-carried between the members of the small group planning the operation. Even the name of the mission was meant to be deceptive to both domestic and foreign observers. The Anadyr is a river flowing into the Bering Sea and also a bomber base in that desolate region of the Soviet Union. Many units scheduled for shipment to Cuba were told to be ready for cold weather and some were even outfitted with skis, felt boots, fleece-lined parkas and other cold weather equipment. The group sent to negotiate with Castro about placing the missiles, including General Ivanov, were sent to Cuba as agricultural experts and technicians. When they arrived in Havana, they were in civilian clothes and had identification papers with false names. Marshal Biryusov, for example, was given the false identity of "Engineer Petrov."

An agreement with Cuba was announced, but it was about the establishment of a civil air route from Moscow to Havana which was a cover, the CIA believed, for shipping in military officers and sensitive equipment. Castro, always willing to make the United States uncomfortable, wanted to announce the military agreements that had been negotiated but Khrushchev refused to allow this. Secrecy was the goal, and it was successfully achieved. (Even when the crisis was over, the original estimates by U. S. intelligence services proved woefully inadequate. Their suppositions were that only 10,000 or so Soviet military personnel were in Cuba when the number was four times that amount.) Once the missiles were in Cuba, the secret was harder to keep. The constant movement of convoys over the limited roadways, the size of the trucks and tractors to haul them to the proposed launch sites, the refusal of the Soviets to allow Cubans to work or live in the immediate areas or even to unload the boats bringing the missiles and equipment to the island aroused suspicions within and without Cuba. The "chatty Cubans" sent a steady stream of clues over the local airwaves and in personal communications which gave an indication of the growing

Soviet presence. And, of course, the network of anti-Castro operatives with ties in the United States supplied an endless stream of intelligence about the construction of the sites and the movement of the missiles. Finally, the constant denials that any offensive weapons were in Cuba by Foreign Minister Andre Gromyko may have tipped off the more savvy of American intelligence officers. The point is, Operation Anadyr was successful in getting the weapons into Cuba and setting up what became the Cuban Missile Crisis.

With the constant flow of human intelligence coming in from the exile community about the possibility of missiles in Cuba and the increased traffic to Cuba from the ships of the Warsaw Pact, the suspicions of the United States were aroused. In August 1962, American officials decided to create two teams of intelligence analysts to review the information that had been gathered to date. One team concentrated on the aerial photographs from recent U-2 flights and other reconnaissance flights over Cuba. The other team reviewed information gained from human intelligence, radio intelligence and other sources. The results of their combined findings were reported by Roger Hilsman, Director of the Bureau of Intelligence and Research at the Department of State. Hilsman disclosed that recent increases in dockings, shipments and coastal activity in Cuba was primarily to strengthen Cuba's coastal defenses but it may have also included the establishment of surface-to-air missile launch sites (SAMs). These were the same type of missiles that had downed U-2 pilot, Francis Gary Powers, flying over the Soviet Union in 1960, much to the embarrassment of the Eisenhower administration which had denied we were flying such missions. This failure, along with a more recent downing of a U-2 over China, made the CIA, which controlled the U-2 program at the time, reluctant to send too many such planes over Cuba. However, the Director of the CIA, John McCone had serious doubts. He was once reported to have stated that they would not put SAMs around the perimeter just to protect cane-cutters and he was right. McCone, a strong anti-communist and ardent Cold Warrior, correctly advised Kennedy that they could only be the prelude to ICBMs or other type of missiles that could reach important bases or cities in the United States. Yet, his own agency and the others reporting to the various services and the NSA failed to follow through. One of the major reasons was the "cry wolf" syndrome of many of the exiles who were reporting the siting of the missiles in Cuba. Far too many had proven false. The U-2 flights were cut back because of the introduction of the SAMs and because of the State Department's worry about another diplomatic disaster such as that with the Powers' downing. In addition, it took a leap of imagination to believe that a rational state, like the U.S.S.R. would actually deploy such weapons into a country run by someone considered mentally unstable by many persons who knew him. For these reasons and more, the United States was not prepared for what the U-2 photographs of October 14, 1962, taken by Major Richard Heyser, showed. On October 16, Kennedy was briefed and shown the damning photographs documenting the establishment of MRBM and IRBM launch sites in Western Cuba. However, in a shrewd diplomatic move, Kennedy waited until after his meeting with Andrei Gromyko, the Soviet foreign minister, who again denied anything like missile installation was going forward, before releasing the findings in his announcement to the nation on October 22. It was the beginning of the most dramatic confrontation of the Cold War or as one historian recently called it, "The Gettysburg of the Cold War."

Kennedy was a traditional Cold Warrior and had grown up in the "containment generation" of foreign policy thinkers and had served with many like-minded men in the House of Representatives and the Senate of the United States. He did not represent a break from the thinking of the past and believed that we had to stand up to our enemies. However, in his first major foreign meeting overseas, he had felt beaten in by Khrushchev at Vienna. Columnist James "Scotty" Reston also reported, ten minutes after Kennedy had his final meeting with Khrushchev, "Khrushchev had studied the events of the Bay of Pigs; he would have understood if Kennedy had left Castro alone or destroyed him; but when Kennedy was rash enough to strike at Cuba but not bold enough to finish the job, Khrushchev decided he was dealing with an inexperienced young leader who could be intimidated and blackmailed. The Communist decision to put offensive missiles into Cuba was the final gamble of this assumption." It was Kennedy's generational belief that communism was a cancer, causing poverty, social upheavals, and economic dislocations, that had to be eradicated. Most of the revolutions of the period were probably of communist origins, he believed, and only a strong, tough United States stood between communism and the free world. Bold actions were needed to suppress the push of the communists. The United States pushed a program of counter-revolution that emphasized economic development, nation building, and modernization. As one who had served in the armed forces and was part of the "Greatest Generation," he believed that the greatest lesson learned from the 1930s was that aggression cannot go unchallenged. To him, Communists and Nazis were the same, with just different labels for oppression. There was little difference between the beliefs of the Eisenhower administration and that of Kennedy except that Kennedy and his cadre were going to be more effective and efficient and constantly active. Force and toughness were to be the bywords of the new administration, even after the fiasco of the Bay of Pigs and his confrontational loss of face at Vienna. The situation in Cuba afforded Kennedy a new opportunity to exhibit his toughness and that of the United States, and the Soviets *would be* forced out of that oppressed island. Now the American public, along with the nation's allies, had to be brought on board.

The start of the crisis came with the discovery of the missiles by U. S. intelligence planes and the men who made the proper evaluation of the information on the film. The key signature of the launch sites' construction, identical to those photographed in the Soviet Union by reconnaissance aircraft, played a major role in determining the inherent danger of the missiles to the United States. Just prior to Kennedy's public announcement of Soviet activities in Cuba on October 22, his team of advisors had contacted our major allies in Europe and obtained their backing, and members of the Organization of American States (OAS) had been appraised of the content of the speech. The media was persuaded to not publish any stories about the discovery until after the speech. Members of the diplomatic corps in Washington were informed about the events about to transpire and most had contacted their home countries before the speech aired. The administration had lined up the support needed to make an impact upon Khrushchev and his colleagues in the Kremlin and in Havana.

The main theme of Kennedy's announcement was simple—the Soviets had to remove the missiles from Cuba. Castro, per se, was not included in any way in the president's speech. The confrontation was between the United States and the Soviet Union, and the instrument chosen by the ExComm (Executive Committee of Kennedy's most trusted advisors) was a "quarantine." The American action against the Soviets was not to be a blockade, since in international law, a blockade was an act of war and that was to be avoided at all costs. The quarantine was to stop all vessels carrying arms and warheads into Cuba, but allow those transporting petroleum, food, medicine, and other vital humanitarian supplies to continue to the island. Debates within the ExComm were intense, and the Joint Chiefs of Staff (JCS) were not pleased with the result, but they obeyed the decisions reached.

Military contingency plans included possible air strikes to take out the missile sites, a possible invasion to overthrow Castro and destroy the missiles, and other variations on this theme, and the JCS assumed that some action would be required militarily. Kennedy, after the Bay of Pigs, was no fan of the military establishment, but wanted the plans and readiness of the military available as options, hoping not to have to use either. In the relationship between Kennedy's civilian government and the military, Kennedy had his hand-picked man, Maxwell Taylor, in place as head of the JCS while his Secretary of Defense, Robert McNamara was in overall charge. Regardless of what Khrushchev believed, Kennedy did not have to worry about a military coup, even when some of his generals disagreed with his choice of methods.

The world watched with bated breath as the two powers squared off as Khrushchev sent his vessels to Cuba across the wide Atlantic to be met, maybe, by the United States Navy. What would happen was anyone's guess. Two important factors were readily known. General Thomas S. Power, the commander of the Strategic Air Command (SAC) broadcast orders to his pilots in clear, English language on more than one occasion, just to let the Soviets know that SAC bombers were always in the air and at the ready. It was announced that SAC was operating at DEFCON 2, and that the next level would bring on an all-out nuclear attack on Soviet installations.

Meetings behind closed doors between Soviet go-betweens and certain members of the administration were taking place almost every day, and they ranged from a member of the KGB contacting John Scali (then working as a television reporter for ABC) to a member of the Soviet diplomatic corps (read intelligence community) meeting with Robert Kennedy negotiating possible flashpoints in efforts to avoid war. Fortunately for the fate of the world, despite the bluster and pomposity Khrushchev displayed to the west and despite the machoism Kennedy put forth toward the east, both were rational men and over the course of the negotiations made attempts to peacefully end the conflict and "save face." For Khrushchev, this was crucial.

The Soviet military was not consulted about or pleased with the situation and were making plans to unseat him (which they accomplished nearly two years later). Kennedy was in the middle of mid-term election campaigns that were critical for his party to maintain control of the House and the Senate. Kennedy had to put aside the fact that he had been lied to by Khrushchev and his diplomats about the militarization of Soviet enclaves in Cuba, and the fact that the latter had turned the island into a forward base both for military purposes and for the promotion of communism in Latin America. As McCone had warned, the build-up of "offensive" weapons in Cuba may not have been just for Cuba's defense against a U. S. invasion, but also as a bargaining chip in Europe for the removal of the Jupiter missiles in Turkey and Italy. Sorting all of this out was the crux of the crisis. Both leaders had a lot to lose in this scenario.

With the twenty-twenty hindsight of today, one can only wonder at why these two rational men ended up putting their nations (and the world) on the brink of nuclear war. It should have been elementary for the Soviets to know that the U-2 program of the CIA would quickly see some of the construction in Cuba, after all, the United States had been flying over the Soviet Union for a number of years. How could the Soviet military allow the construction of the missile sites in Cuba that so closely resembled those in the Soviet Union and not expect U. S. intelligence to spot the similarities? The utter lack of concealment of some of the sites early on was a dead giveaway for even the least trained photo analyst. The forty-thousand troops and other personnel under General Issa Pliyev's command were impossible to ignore, yet CIA/NSA analysis only accounted for ten thousand additional Soviet personnel. The questions simply beg for more obvious answers. One of the few saving graces from the Soviet side was the fact that total control of the nuclear weapons on the island was under strict Soviet control with approval from Moscow needed to use even the Luna tactical weapons in case of an invasion. The fact that nuclear armed weapons were secretly sent to Cuba was totally missed by U. S. intelligence operatives. It was not until a meeting in Moscow in January 1989 that General Anatoly Gribkov confirmed to Robert McNamara that nuclear weapons had indeed been sent to Cuba, the first time the former Secretary of Defense had absolute proof of it. This revelation put Kennedy's decision not to go after the SAM sites, regardless of the advice of the JCSs (and that of McNamara at the beginning of the crisis) into a totally new light. Was this great leadership showing patience or simply luck? What was also even more frightening is the fact that the Single Integrated Operational Plan for Fiscal Year 1962 (SIOP-62) was quite rigid and did not allow for necessary changes to meet the contingency of a war. McNamara expressed his concern in a memorandum to Kennedy noting, "I am convinced that we would not be able to achieve tactical surprise, especially in the kinds of crisis circumstances in which a first-strike capability might be relevant. Thus, the Soviets would be able to launch some of their retaliatory forces before we had destroyed their bases." This kind of report would awaken any rational human to the ever-present dangers of an accidental war, something both Kennedy and Khrushchev realized.

Khrushchev was a pragmatist and not a die-hard ideologue. He believed in rational solutions and thought others, including Kennedy, were of a like mind. Yes, he was known as an impulsive man given to quick decisions, but he was a realist who also knew he was constantly being watched by his enemies in the Kremlin. He was aware of the failures of some of his agricultural programs, which left the Soviet Union dependent upon foreign shipments of wheat and other foodstuffs. Khrushchev was cognizant also of the weaknesses of the Soviet missile program, despite its spectacular success with Sputnik. The missile gap was a burden on the Soviet economy too, because the arsenal of the United States outnumbered it by an estimated 15-1 ratio and the Soviet delivery system took much longer to set up and fire than anything the U.S. had at the time. He was also aware of Great Britain's Thor program, which became operational during the middle of this crisis. Khrushchev was in a relatively weak position in October 1962, but he needed to "win" something out of the crisis to keep his critics at bay. In the end, Khrushchev got that with the secret/delayed agreement to have the United States remove its outdated Jupiters from Turkey and Italy. He also got Kennedy to agree to an ambiguous "no invasion' pledge to satisfy Castro, a man both men considered non-rational. The joint fear of an accidental starting of war plagued both leaders and led to the final "settlement" of the Cuban Missile Crisis on October 28-29, 1962. The last vessels were ordered to turn around and, in November, the missile sites were dismantled. The final removal of the outdated LL28s actually marked the end of the crisis for the Soviets and the

United States. Kennedy did get his wish, Castro was excluded from the final settlement or having any say in it. Khrushchev was left with the task of trying to mollify his ally, who felt totally betrayed by his recent protector/friend. It was a pragmatic conclusion to a difficult situation.

The solution may have been pragmatic on both sides, but the impact on the Sunshine State was anything but subtle. During the crisis over 100,000 troops were sent to bases in Florida and the Southeast ready to assist in the proposed invasion of Cuba. Twenty-four tactical air wings were also added to the arsenal already stationed at Florida's air bases. The constant stream of convoys of men and equipment tied up traffic throughout the state and temporarily hindered the tourist from entering the state. The eastern coast of Florida was flooded with men, equipment, and expectations. Civil Defense became a by-word with the state's government as Governor Farris Bryant figured greatly in both state and national planning of CD. Of course, the economy benefited from the large influx of military expenditures and created a demand for a better, improved infrastructure. Afterwards, President Kennedy made two nationally covered trips to Florida to award various installations for their service during the crisis, adding his newly garnered prestige to the state's position in national and international affairs. Every section of the state was affected by the crisis, but in different ways. The essays that follow show just how unique each area in Florida was at the height of the nation's and world's most dangerous crisis of the 20th Century. The essays are also testaments to the fortitude of Florida citizens in a post-World War II world.

ABBREVIATED BIBLIOGRAPHY

Manuel E. Falcon. "Bay of Pigs and Cuban Missile Crisis: Presidential Decision Making and Its Effect on Military Employment During the Kennedy Administration." U. S. Army Command and General Staff College, Fort Leavenworth, Kansas, 1993.

Michael R. Beschloss. *The Crisis Years: Kennedy and Khruschev, 1960-1963.* New York: Edward Burlingame Books, 1991.

Nikita Khrushchev (Introduction and notes by Edward Crankshaw). *Khrushchev Remembers.* Boston: Little, Brown and Company, 1970. 458-460.

Elie Abel. *The Missile Crisis.* Philadelphia: J. P. Lippincott Company, 1966.

Robert F. Kennedy. *Thirteen Days: A Memoir of the Cuban Missile Crisis.* New York: W. W. Norton, 1969.

Richard Helms (With William Hood). *A Look Over My Shoulder: A Life in the Central Intelligence Agency.* New York: Ballantine Books, 2003.

CHAPTER 1

Mystery in the Skies: Orlando's McCoy Air Force Base and the Cuban Missile Crisis

BY JOY WALLACE DICKINSON

"People buying gas and people having their cars worked on at the filling stations came out to applaud the soldiers in the convoy. I can remember the fear. No, it was more anxiety than fear."

Shirleen Rutig

So many planes—that's what many longtime Orlandoans remember first about the Cuban Missile Crisis. My brother, Bill, was only 8 years old in October 1962, but the memory is razor sharp for him: row upon row of monster aircraft sailing high over the lake in front of our house. Author Susan Carol McCarthy, who grew up in the Orlando area, painted the picture in her novel *A Place We Knew Well*, as she described B-52 bombers from McCoy Air Force Base looming above the city's College Park neighborhood. With them is a huge Stratotanker, its refueling boom "retracted like a scorpion's stinger at rest." The ground trembled from the jet power passing overhead.

McCarthy's well-researched story, set during the crisis, is fiction, but the bombers were very real. So was McCoy, the Strategic Air Command base that was a source of pride for Orlandoans and part of a heritage that linked the city with military aviation. For Orlando, McCoy was central to Cuban Missile Crisis. About 11 miles south of downtown, the base began during World War II as the Pinecastle Army Air Field—a name inspired by the historic community of Pine Castle. In the 1870s, journalist Will Wallace Harney had arrived from Kentucky and built a notable frontier home dubbed the "pine castle," and soon the area around Harney was called that as well. The location of the air base was actually several miles south of Pine Castle, which continues to be rendered as two words, while the name of the base was one word: Pinecastle. Such are the quirks of history's details.

However it was spelled, the Pinecastle Army Air Field was surrounded by plenty of piney scrub. It was Orlando's second World War II base, carved into a sandspur-strewn patch of city-owned land in 1941, before Pearl Harbor. It supported Orlando Army Air Base, which opened in September 1940 when the Army Air Corps took over the city's municipal airport east of downtown and converted it into a training center for pilots and fighter and bomber groups. Thousands of troops were stationed there during the war. When the Pinecastle facility was added to support Orlando's training mission, it was originally designated Orlando Air Army Air Field No. 2 and renamed Pinecastle Army Air Field on January 1, 1943. At least one serviceman who was transferred there remembered it as nothing "but the runway and a bunch of tents." And there might be cows on the runway.

With the longest ranching history of any state in the union, Florida was also the last state to pass a mandatory fencing law, in 1949. If a cow ambled across the road and a car ran into it, the driver was at fault. This meant that throughout World War II and for several years afterward, cows from neighboring pastureland would wander onto the runway at

Pinecastle or into hangars, sometimes startling pilots coming in for a landing or mechanics working on planes.

"The problem was worse when it was cold because the cattle would congregate on the warm runway where the concrete held the heat," Don Lancaster, whose grandfather bought the land next to the Pinecastle field in 1939, told the *Orlando Sentinel* in 1995. The cows would also sleep on the runway at night because of the warmth the concrete retained from the day's sun. "For a time, it was the job of some of the airmen to scan the field with binoculars to see if any cattle were on or near the runway when a plane was getting ready to take off or land, and they would rush out in trucks to chase away our cows," Lancaster said. "Officers at the base would call our house to complain loudly about the cattle. My father and uncle would get on their horses, round up the strays, and push them back to the south onto our property."

The Lancasters' cows had some interesting action to watch. Even after the drawdown of wartime airfields began in 1945, various aircraft continued to be tested at Pinecastle. In January 1946, its remote location and 10,000-foot runway, one of the nation's longest, brought an exceptional mission to the base. Bell Aircraft Corporation began secret test flights on its rocket-powered X-1 supersonic aircraft—the same craft in which Chuck Yeager would make history 21 months later by flying faster than sound over a dry California lake bed in October 1947.

On January 25, 1946, the X-1 made its maiden flight over Central Florida, gliding minus its rocket engine over the lake-dotted landscape. Dropped from the bomb bay of a B-29 Superfortress flying at 25,000 feet, the sleek, saffron-colored aircraft dropped more steeply than its 29-year-old test pilot, Jack Woolams, expected—barely clearing a row of trees and touching down 400 feet short of the runway. It rolled the length of three football fields before stopping. The time: 9 minutes, 42 seconds. No doubt the cows were amazed.

Despite the bumpy landing, neither Woolams nor the top-secret plane were hurt in the maiden flight of the X-1, and Woolams would glide in it and land at Pinecastle nine more times during the next six weeks before the tests were moved to Muroc Dry Lake in California (now Edwards Air Force Base), where the rocket engine was installed. The X-1 team made the move to the remote California desert for a variety of reasons, including secrecy for the highly classified project. But the X-1 would not be the last secret plane landing on the long runway in the midst of Florida's cattle country, as Orlandoans would learn years later during the Cuban Missile Crisis.

With X-1 testing moving to California and defense cutbacks following the war, the military formally returned the Pinecastle base to the city of Orlando in July 1947. But the military's hiatus at the base would be short. In September 1947, the Air Force was made a separate branch of the U.S. military, and in June 1948, it reactivated Pinecastle as part of an expansion program and also added a radar school at Orlando Air Force Base. Soon, 6,000 troops began to arrive at Pinecastle. For Orlando, a city of about 37,000 before World War II, these bases loomed large, and during the Korean War and the Cold War in the 1950s, they loomed even larger.

In April 1951, the Air Force confirmed that the reactivated base south of Orlando would be a training station for B-47 bomber combat crews. Officially declared Pinecastle Air Force Base in September 1951, it underwent a $100 million construction program that lengthened the existing north-south runway and added a parallel runway, making both more than 2 miles long. Flight training began in early 1952. At the end of 1953, the Air Force transferred the B-47 training mission at the base from its Air Training Command to the Strategic Air Command. The next year, 1954, Orlando leaders thought the city had such a strong association with the Air Force that they made a bid for the proposed U.S. Air Force Academy but lost out to Colorado Springs.

Also in 1954, the Air Force transferred Colonel Michael N. W. McCoy—the unofficial dean of SAC's B-47 Stratojet aircraft commanders—from MacDill Air Force Base in Tampa to Pinecastle, where he would command the 321st Bombardment Wing. McCoy's life in Orlando, short as it was, and his dramatic death three years later, brought the base to even more prominence in the awareness of many Orlandoans. Indeed, the crash in which McCoy died still holds an important place in Orlando lore. On October 9, 1957, which was McCoy's 52nd birthday, the B-47 Stratojet he was piloting passed over the city's College Park neighborhood and crashed near Ben White Raceway, killing all on board: in addition to McCoy, Group Captain John Woodroffe of the Royal Air Force and two officers of the 321st, Lieutenant Colonel Charles Joyce and Major Vernon D. Stuff. Just days before, on October 4, the Soviet Union had launched Sputnik, "the first earth satellite ever put in globe-girdling orbit under man's controls," as the *Orlando Sentinel* described it, ratcheting up the Cold War and the race into space.

News stories depicted McCoy as a hero who had steered the doomed bomber away from homes and schools before it exploded. Not one person on the ground "was even scratched by the tremendous explosion," the *Sentinel* reported, describing McCoy as "a dominating figure in Orlando's civic life" and "a living legend." By 1957, he had logged more flying time than anyone in the Air Force—20,000 hours, beginning in the 1920s with barnstorming flights in World War I-era "Jennies." McCoy had set a B-47 speed record from London to the United States. When he climbed into a plane, his custom was to lift a clenched fist and yell "Charge." Orlandoans had embraced him, and he had christening his chief plane the "City of Orlando." According to the *Sentinel* after his death, "the warrior flier with a great heart went out fighting to protect the people of the city he loved." After his death, Pinecastle Air Force Base was renamed McCoy Air Force Base in 1958.

Over the years, though, some Orlandoans repeated rumors that McCoy in the cockpit was "the hot dog from hell," a daredevil who had flown too fast, perhaps to show off to the visiting RAF officer. In 2007, an investigation by Sentinel reporter Kevin Spear unearthed previously un-released evidence that the Air Force did in fact swiftly blame McCoy for the tragedy, if not for the same reasons the rumors proposed. "The records conclude that one of the nation's premier military fliers somehow had a brief lapse of control in an unforgiving plane," Spear wrote, citing Air Force records that had been classified for 50 years. "It was a Cold War incident kept shrouded in secrecy from even families of the dead."

McCoy commanded a fleet of nearly 50 B-47s at Pinecastle. Although the B-47 never saw major combat, 464 crewmen died in crashes between 1951 and 1966. "In level flight and lightly loaded, an inattentive pilot could accelerate the bomber until it ripped itself apart," Spear wrote, while high speeds could flex the wings so wildly that the pilot lost control. "If you relaxed for a minute, it would turn around and bite you," retired Colonel Sigmund Alexander, a B-47 veteran, told Spear. Almost four years after McCoy's death, a reorganization began at McCoy Air Force Base in summer 1961 to convert the base from the B-47 Stratojets to B-52 "Stratofortress" heavy bombers. The 321st Bomb Wing was deactivated in October 1961.

Near the base, Orlandoans welcomed another major link to the space age and the Cold War when the Glenn L. Martin Company (later Martin Marietta and now part of Lockheed Martin) opened its new Orlando plant in December 1957, just a couple of months after McCoy's dramatic death. In 1955, Martin had announced plans to move its production and all its engineers to Orlando from Baltimore, Md.— an event that some have called as significant in the city's development as the arrival of Walt Disney World in 1971. In 1957, Martin was building the Vanguard booster rocket, which would launch some of the first U.S. satellites into orbit, along with ballistic missiles for the military, and it needed a manufacturing facility close to Cape Canaveral, about 54 miles to the east on the Atlantic Coast. By 1961, the company, now known as the Martin Marietta Corporation, was Florida's single largest employer, with about 10,500 people working in 23 buildings south of Orlando.

Increasingly, Orlandoans saw themselves as deeply connected to the nation's burgeoning space program as well as its system of military defense. A group of young movers and shakers even began the annual Missile Bowl, which pitted top teams from U.S. military services in a pageant of pigskin glory and patriotism. The teams consisted primarily of fine college players who had been drafted into the armed services. The first Missile Bowl, on December 3, 1960, pitted the Quantico Marines against the Pensacola Navy Goshawks before a crowd of 7,000 in Orlando's Tangerine Bowl. The Department of Defense had always made it clear that, should a military crisis arise, the bowl might be cancelled. That never happened, but it almost did—a couple of years later, during the Cuban Missile Crisis.

The dates usually given for the Cuban Missile Crisis, the famous "thirteen days"—are October 16 through October 28, 1962. But perhaps it really began on Sunday, October 14, when Major Richard Heyser climbed into the cockpit of a U-2 spy plane in the California desert and headed for Cuba. The high-resolution images Heyser took as he soared 70,000 feet over the island's western edge would start the United States on the road to a direct confrontation with the Soviet Union. At the time, Heyser saw the flight as routine. After he landed at McCoy Air Force Base at Orlando and his film was sent to Washington, Heyser took a shower and headed to church. The next day, when CIA analysts studied his film, they found evidence of Soviet medium-range ballistic missiles in Cuba. Eight days later, on the evening of Monday, October 22, President John F. Kennedy told the nation on live television that the Soviets were installing nuclear missiles just 90 miles from Key West. Capable of striking most cities in the United States, they would be operational soon.

Today, Heyser and Major Rudolf Anderson Jr. are credited with being the two U-2 pilots who took the first photographs that showed ballistic missile bases under construction in Cuba. They were also the first two pilots sent to Orlando from Laughlin Air Force Base in Texas in early October 1962 to fly the specially equipped U-2 planes over Cuba. Subsequent flights by Anderson provided further details—until he was shot down by missiles over Cuba on Saturday, October 27. The only person to be killed by enemy fire during the crisis, Anderson had not been scheduled to fly on the day of the mission, but he lobbied hard for the assignment when the mission was added to the schedule and took off from McCoy. (Although Anderson was the only combat death, the Cuban Missile Crisis did have other casualties: three RB-47 Stratojets crashed between September 27 and November 11, killing a total of 11 crew members, and seven more airmen died when a C-135B Stratolifter delivering ammunition to Naval Station Guantanamo Bay crashed on approach on October 23.)

Nicknamed "The Dragon Lady," the U-2 had zoomed into public awareness in May 1960, when the Soviet Union shot down one of the high-flying spy planes in Soviet air space and captured its pilot, Francis Gary Powers, who was sentenced to 10 years in prison but released in exchange for a captured Soviet agent after he served less than two years. That incident had raised tensions between the United States and the Soviet Union, but now, in October 1962, they were about to reach the boiling point, and although the U-2 flights over Cuba were deeply clandestine and secrecy reigned about the strange comings and goings at McCoy, the appearance of two U-2s at McCoy got Orlandoans' attention.

"Residents have reported the presence of at least two U-2 spy planes which have been based at McCoy for nearly a week," the *Orlando Sentinel's* Charlie Wadsworth reported on October 24. "Stern-visaged spokesmen again refused comment last night and continued to wrap a heavy cloak of tightened security measures around increased activity at McCoy Air Force Base." But it was obvious that something was up. Some residents had reported evidence of the buildup the previous week, but it wasn't until the Sunday afternoon of October 21—a week after Heyser took pictures over Cuba—"that it became rather noisily apparent that something was going on at McCoy."

The sky over the Orlando area roared with the sound of jet engines, and "the drone of an endless procession of troop carriers and cargo planes could be heard." Residents also reported seeing two of the Air Force's top-performing fighter planes at McCoy, Wadsworth noted. When pressed, McCoy officials had acknowledged the presence of additional aircraft at the base, explaining that they were Tactical Air Command planes engaged in a training exercise at McCoy. Then, at mid-morning on Monday, October 22, "the Air Force switched signals and adopted its 'no comment' attitude," clamping a lid of secrecy on everything. Also on Monday, McCoy police had arrested Walt Mack, a 27-year-old *Sentinel* reporter, and had searched his car and confiscated his camera and film. He was released after about an hour of questioning, but his film was not. And at the same time that base officials refused comment, sleek F-100 and F-105 fighter planes "continued to land and take off at regular intervals," Wadsworth wrote. Officials at nearby Patrick Air Force Base in Cocoa Beach were more forthcoming, he added; they had said that extra aircraft were "part of the backup for the U.S. blockade of Cuba." But Patrick, too, had "tightened its security belt."

Secrecy was tight at McCoy as well. Bud Grierson, then a B-52 commander, recalled 25 years later that on October 22, waves of C-119 aircraft began landing at McCoy, loaded with paratroopers. "I thought, 'What the hell is going on,'" Grierson said in 1987. "This is a SAC base, and you didn't see paratroopers at a SAC base." In a couple of days, Grierson and other B-52 fliers were gathered together and told "to go home for an hour and say hello to our wives and pack and come back." The Air Force was sending McCoy's B-52s to other bases such as Turner Air Force Base in Albany, Georgia, and Sheppard Field in Wichita Falls, Texas, to make room at McCoy for more Army paratroopers, who could be dropped into Cuba for an invasion. The B-52s were gone for about six weeks and began flying 24-hour missions so that they would be in the air if they were needed to launch an attack under orders from the president. On those missions, the B-52s "were loaded with nukes," Grierson recalled. "We would go over to Spain and pick up tankers there, refuel, then head out to about Corsica, then turn around and come back into a long racetrack orbit to the western end of Gibraltar and the eastern end of the Mediterranean, pick up another tanker, pick up some more fuel, then head back to the states."

Back in Central Florida, sleek jet fighters roared in every few minutes at McCoy for possible duty in a confrontation with the Soviets. In addition to the planes crowding the skies, southbound military convoys jammed major highways—another clear memory for many Central Floridians. "I thought to myself, 'Oh, God, we're going to war,'" Shirleen Rutig recalled 30 years later. She arrived at this conclusion after watching a convoy from the gas station where she had stopped. "People buying gas and people having their cars worked on at the filling stations came out to applaud the soldiers in the convoy," Rutig said. "I can remember the fear. No, it was more anxiety than fear," she said.

The public didn't know much in part because of the secrecy, but also it's important to remember that 1962 was a different time than today in terms of media coverage. Now, an event like the Cuban Missile Crisis would be greeted with 24-hour coverage on multiple television networks, complete with its own logo. But in 1962, TV was far from around-the-clock—stations signaled the end the broadcast day with the national anthem, followed by a test pattern. When President Kennedy asked for television time from all three broadcast networks (ABC, CBS, NBC) for 7 p.m. on Monday, October 22, for a speech to the nation demanding that the Soviets remove all missiles from Cuba, his address signaled a major event not only in the history of the Cold War and also in the evolution of television, according to the Paley Center for Media.

Watching on a black-and-white TV in Orlando, "I sat there paralyzed," former Florida Senator Melquíades "Mel" Martinez recalls in his autobiography, *A Sense of Belonging*—the story of his journey from Cuban émigré teenager to government leader. Martinez, then a student at Orlando's Bishop Moore Catholic High School, turned 16 on October 23, 1962, the day after Kennedy's speech. He was living with the Orlando family of Walter and Eileen Young and had only been in Florida since the previous summer, when he had fled Cuba along with thousands of other unaccompanied Cuban minors as part of Operation Pedro Pan. Between 1960 and 1962, the program, created by the Catholic Welfare Bureau of Miami, airlifted more than 14,000 Cuban children from Havana to the United States. For them, the Cuban Missile Crisis was especially terrifying.

"As though it were yesterday, I can recall every detail of sitting in the living room with the Youngs" and watching President Kennedy, Martinez wrote. "Well, this is it," he recalls Walter Young, saying. "This is World War III." "My God," Eileen Young replied after a moment of silence, "The world is going to end." Martinez thought of his parents, little sister, grandmothers, his whole extended family in Cuba, "they were all at ground zero for Armageddon." And as the crisis unfolded, the outcome was increasingly bitter for Cubans like Martinez, who had hoped that their exile would be brief, that Castro would be vanquished, and that they would be reunited with their families back home.

Historian José B. Fernández, former dean of the College of Arts and Humanities at the University of Central Florida in Orlando, was fourteen years old during the crisis and had come to Florida through Operation Pedro Pan also. Years later he recalled that "in the Cuban neighborhood of Miami, everybody was saying, 'We're all going home within two days. This is the end of Fidel. The Americans are going to make up for the Bay of Pigs and bomb the island.'" But as the crisis unfolded, the young exiles faced a "nightmare scenario," as Martinez describes it. "Watching the Cuban Missile Crisis in real time, I was forced to confront hard realities. I might be on my own in this life indefinitely. My family's dislocation could last forever." (After four years of separation, the Martinez family was reunited in Florida in 1966.)

For Cuban-Americans who lived through the crisis in Florida, "the sense that we were wronged still haunts many of us," journalist Myriam Marquez wrote in the *Orlando Sentinel* in 1992, at the 30th anniversary of the crisis. Born in Havana, Marquez left Cuba with her family when she was a small child. Now executive editor of *el Nuevo Herald* in Miami, she was on the *Sentinel's* editorial board when she described the Cuban community's sense of betrayal in 1962, when her father had wondered, "Why would the powerful United States let a two-bit communist run a country just 90 miles away from Florida?" "Many Cuban-Americans still are repulsed by the Democratic Party because of what happened 30 years ago," Marquez wrote in 1992—words that may still be true today.

Cuban émigré families were surely at the epicenter of the crisis. "Everyone my age can vividly reconstruct the tense days of October 1962 as the Cuban Missile Crisis unfolded," Martinez writes in this autobiography. But for some of us who grew up Florida during the 1950s, memories of the crisis may be less vivid—in part, perhaps, because we were self-absorbed American teens in 1962 but also because we had grown up under a cloak of fear. Like Martinez, I remember watching President Kennedy on television and I remember being worried about it, but these memories are mixed with the general sense of worry that pervaded growing up in Orlando during the Cold War.

Certainly as many Orlandoans look back at the Cuban Missile Crises, they remember the confusion and fear. Grace Chewning, who was then secretary to the City Council, recalls that "City Hall was being stocked up with supplies to be a city emergency control center" and that a colonel from McCoy Air Force Base was at City Hall almost every day. "The mayor and City Council were debating whether or not to declare a state of emergency," recalls Chewning, who went on to serve as Orlando's city clerk for a half-century. "We had to put extra people on to handle all the building permits for bomb shelters."

But if you scan the city's daily newspaper during the crisis, you may be more impressed by how low-profile the crisis appears, especially contrasted with the way news is delivered today. Those bomb shelters they were scrambling to permit at City Hall seem to have been more the result of old-fashioned sales efforts than of advertising or news reports, for example. "I didn't much think about what might be going on until the bomb-shelter salesman showed up at our door," Orlandoan Sally Grant recalled later. "During his sales pitch, he just about scared me to death."

Many Orlandoans surely must have been scared by headlines such as "Washington Engulfed in Air of Crisis," the lead headline on October 22—the day Kennedy spoke on TV later in the evening—but that Monday, the air of crisis was competing for Orlandoans' attention with the grand opening of the expanded Colonial Plaza, "the largest and newest shopping complex south of Atlanta," with 3,000 new parking places and a mall capped by a four-story Jordan Marsh department store. In opening ceremonies that morning, eleven beauty queens from neighboring communities snipped a ribbon, and "one of the biggest shopping sprees in the history of Orlando was under way," the *Sentinel* reported.

On the editorial page the next day, the paper's powerful editor and publisher Martin Andersen backed President Kennedy's "strong and irrevocable stand on Cuba and the Communist menace," a view supported by residents who were interviewed for a follow-up article on October 24. "I think we should have invaded them a long time ago," said Clarence Mullins, a Winter Park utility worker—a sentiment echoed by several of those interviewed. "After we sink a couple of Russian ships, everything's gonna be all right," noted Orlandoan George Sanders. But some people felt more queasy than bellicose. "We live right next to McCoy," said Mrs. L. J. Henderson. "My husband served 14 months overseas. "I hate to see it, but I don't know what else to do. It just makes me feel sick all over. I have a son, 19, too."

By Saturday, October 27, Orlando's ninth annual Parade of Homes was competing for front-page space with the latest from Kennedy and Krushchev. That same day, Charlie Wadsworth, who had reported about the secrecy at McCoy earlier in the week, repeated Senator George Smathers' take on the situation in Wadsworth's popular "Hush Puppies" column. Krushchev had hoped to sneak his medium-range missiles into Cuba under cover of Hurricane Ella in mid-October, Wadsworth wrote, also citing speculation that the Soviets had hauled their mid-range missiles to Cuba to threaten the U.S because their long-range missiles—"the highly propagandized ICBM's"—were "inferior to U.S. systems." These observers were certainly "not saying that Russia does not have any long-range missiles," Wadsworth added. "They know better."

So did many Central Floridans, including schoolchildren. Whether bombs might arrive by plane or missile, we knew that the shadow of nuclear war hung over us, and that, because of all the military installations in the state, including McCoy Air Force Base, we had been in the crosshairs long before the Cuban Missile Crisis. As Gary Mormino writes in his social history of Florida, *Land of Sunshine, State of Dreams*," the Cold War "touched the most familiar and remote areas of Florida."

The 1950s and early 1960s are often depicted as cheery time when bobbysoxers in poodle skirts danced to "Rock Around the Clock." But some postwar pop songs included lines such as: "A mushroom cloud hangs over my dreams. It haunts my future and threatens my schemes." If your taste runs to gospel, you may know the Louvin Brothers' 1952 classic that begins, "Are you ready for the great atomic power? Will you rise and meet your Savior in the air?"

Well before the Cuban Missile Crisis, Orlandoans lived under the shadow of the Bomb—the atomic-powered means to the end of the world. After August 29, 1949, when the Soviet Union shocked the U.S. with proof that it too had the Bomb, "suddenly the world had two ideologically opposed countries with the capability of unleashing unprecedented devastation upon each other," Matt Novak writes on his blog, *Paleofuture*. "The campaign to mobilize average Americans by normalizing the discussion of collective death (even with children) was under way." Good citizens rallied to the call of public-service ads like one that began, "Hi! This is Tony Bennett! Make sure you're prepared if a nuclear attack ever comes!"

Well before 1962, Floridians busied ourselves building bomb shelters and designing school civil-defense drills. My parents—usually sticklers for adherence to rules and regulations—did not embrace my elementary school's evacuation plans. If the mushroom-cloud crisis came, I was told not to get on the buses or cars that authorities hoped would carry schoolchildren to safety. Instead, I was instructed to walk to my grandparents' house, near the school, and our family would at least be together.

Even more bizarre than escape by carpool was the early Cold War practice of issuing metal dog tags to schoolchildren. We got them one year at Orlando's Hillcrest Elementary in the 1950s. I had no idea of their real purpose—to identify bodies after an attack. I just vaguely knew that my dad had dog tags in World War II and somehow by association I thought they were cool. Unfortunately, I parted with my tags years ago, but my friend Sherry Meadows Lewis still has her set from another Orlando elementary school, Audubon Park. Some other school districts also issued dog tags elsewhere in the country in the early 1950s, in cities that were considered likely targets of attack.

Floridians had other reminders of the Bomb, too, before the Cuban Missile Crisis. Pat Frank's apocalyptic novel *Alas, Babylon*, published in

1959, was widely read in Orlando and elsewhere in Florida. Set in Fort Repose, a fictional town modeled on Mount Dora, the novel depicts the bombing of airbases that turns Central Florida into a "contaminated zone." A *Playhouse 90* television adaptation was broadcast on April 3, 1960, and starred Don Murray, Burt Reynolds, and Rita Moreno. In the book, the brother of the protagonist, Randy Bragg, is a colonel in the U.S. Air Force intelligence service and asks Bragg to meet him during a layover at McCoy Air Force Base. The base named for the legendary Colonel McCoy was never far from Orlandoans' awareness of the Cold War and their place in it. Indeed, the base seemed to enjoy special relationship with the city.

"McCoy was different from a lot of bases," former B-52 crew chief John Blalock recalled in 1986, as McCoy veterans planned a reunion. "It was where people wanted to retire." Blalock, like many Orlando-area residents, attributed the great rapport between the city and the base to the base's best-known commander, the hard-charging pilot for whom it was named. During his time in Orlando, McCoy had played an avid role as a community activist, advocating for the widening of highways, organizing community cleanup programs, and working with children. An Orlando elementary school bears his name, and the letters "MCO" remain the official code for what the base eventually became: Orlando International Airport.

That transformation began even before the Cuban Missile Crisis, with three years of negotiations that culminated in January 1964 with the Air Force's agreement to a permanent lease for a civilian jetport at McCoy. In December 1965, the city set up a fund to prepare McCoy for full commercial use by May 21, 1966. When the Department of Defense announced in mid-April 1973 that McCoy Air Force Base would close, it was also announced that the city of Orlando would acquire the $61 million facility for jetport expansion. The base was officially closed in June 1974. Carl Langford, Orlando's mayor from 1967 to 1980, considered that his most significant achievement had been negotiating the city's purchase of McCoy for one dollar, Langford's obituary noted in 2011. Now Orlando International Airport is one of the nation's largest airports, serving more than 42 million passengers annually. At 21 square miles, it's the fourth largest airport in the United States in terms of land mass.

In a corner of the airport, just off the Beachline Expressway (the former Bee Line) near runway 18L, B-52 Memorial Park pays tribute to the history of that land. It's a compact, relatively hidden park under the control of the Greater Orlando Aviation Authority, dedicated in 1985 to members of the 306th Bomb Wing and Strategic Air Command who served at McCoy Air Force Base between 1957 and 1974. The park's main feature is a retired B-52D Stratofortress, Air Force Serial Number 56-0687, that was built in 1956 and retired in 1984. It's just the kind of plane that would fly across the Atlantic during the Cuban Missile Crisis on nuke-laden, 24-hour missions designed to make the Soviets nervous. Returning from such a mission, "We'd get out and kiss the ground," retired Air Force Colonel William G. Walker recalled in 2001.

Eventually the B-52s would return to their home at McCoy Air Force Base, where cows had invaded the runway during World War II and the experimental X-1 glided in for secret landings in 1946. Now, in October 1962, sleek spy planes took off for Cuba from McCoy and fighter pilots pored over maps of Cuban targets. "It was tense," retired Air Force Major Joe Demes said in 2001 as he prepared for a McCoy veterans' reunion. "The public didn't know how close we were to war. We knew if somebody coughed, that would be it." Then, the crisis was over, and Demes "was home before Christmas, building a home in Orlando." Everything was back to normal, but for his family and many others, "this was the closest we ever came" to war.

ABBREVIATED BIBLIOGRAPHY

Bacon, Eve. *Orlando: A Centennial History* (Chuluota, Florida: Mickler House, 1977), Vol. II.

Frank, Pat. *Alas, Babylon* (Philadelphia: J. B. Lippincott, 1959).

McCarthy, Susan Carol. *A Place We Knew Well: A Novel* (New York: Bantam Books-Random House, 2015).

Martinez, Mel, with Ed Breslin. *A Sense of Belonging: From Castro's Cuba to the U.S. Senate, One Man's Pursuit of the American Dream* (New York: Crown Forum, 2008).

Miller, Jay. *Lockheed U-2 (Aerograph 3)* (Tulsa, Okla., Aerofax, Inc., 1993).

Orlando Sentinel, microfilm records, Orlando Public Library.

Orlando Sentinel files at Newsbank.com, available through the Orange County Library System.

CHAPTER 2

The Cuban Missile Crisis: Along the Space Coast

BY NICK WYNNE

"I remember the fear and concern as we had to practice at school in case of a missile strike. I remember us having to close all the windows in the classroom and then hiding under our desks. It was a scary time for me, as we knew my mother was fearful, so we were too."

Judy Clifton Steighner

The 1960s ushered in a new decade of hope and change for residents along Florida's Space Coast. Although the Russians had beaten the United States in launching a satellite into Earth orbit in October 1957 and had also successfully put the first astronaut into space in April 1961, the U.S. was pouring money into its space program at Cape Canaveral. Thousands of new residents flooded into the areas along the Atlantic coast from New Smyrna Beach to Indian River County. As a group, these new residents were educated, highly paid, and eager to become permanent residents of this quaint and picturesque section of the Sunshine State. The region's economy also grew as housing construction boomed, as new businesses were born, and as cities enjoyed phenomenal growth. Schools, churches, restaurants, night clubs, and a myriad of other new enterprises seemingly emerged like wild mushrooms after a summer rain, growing overnight and springing up full blown, ready to serve an ever increasing public.

Floridians had experienced similar "booms" in the past—during the 1920s and World War II—but this boom was different. The space program was based on new and developing technology and its workers were highly educated. Civic leaders pointed with pride to the program and informed long-time residents that the space program was simply the harbinger of greater things to come. In their vision, new industries and manufacturing plants, employing thousands of workers, replaced the rambling citrus packing houses and numerous citrus groves. Small towns—Titusville, Cocoa, Cocoa Beach, and Melbourne—suddenly promoted themselves as the centers of the space program. So promising was the region's future that the General Development Corporation spent millions of dollars creating a new town, Palm Bay, out of thousands of acres of worthless scrub land. Astronauts-in-training added to the general "go-go-go" atmosphere of the region when they cavorted in local night clubs and drove their donated Corvettes recklessly in the streets. The astronauts who became out-of-touch heroes to the rest of the world were fully integrated into the Brevard County community, although somewhat removed because of their prominent status.

Along the beaches, Gus Edwards' long ignored Cocoa Beach development became the center of the new social scene that saw the multitude of night clubs and restaurants along Highway A1A play host to celebrities like Walter Cronkite, Werner von Braun, and countless other famous people. Also along the beaches, a burgeoning surfing culture began to take root as outsiders introduced the "California lifestyle" to locals. Among those that rode the longboards along the Atlantic was Jack Roland Murphy, who, in 1963, would achieve infamy as "Murph the Surf, the man who stole the Star of India sapphire."

First incorporated in 1925 and reincorporated in 1959, Cocoa Beach enjoyed a major boom during the decade of the 1960s, as evidenced by the construction in 1960-61 of a major branch of the First Federal Savings and Loan Association. Known as the "Glass Bank" because of its all glass exterior walls, the bank building became an immediate tourist attraction and symbolized the Cocoa Beach spirit—new, different, and, above all, exciting!

In other parts of the United States, citizens looked longingly at the frenzied development of the Space Coast. The traditional centers of manufacturing and industrial wealth were quickly turning into the "Rust Belt" as old technology of iron and steel could not keep up with the newly emerging of computers and satellites. The space program brought together a large group of highly educated, well paid, and very cosmopolitan individuals, ready to conquer outer space and change the world. Their impact on local culture and society was immediate and long lasting. County authorities and city leaders began to fund new infrastructure improvements to handle the demands of a rapidly exploding population; contractors and developers began to create entirely new subdivisions and shopping centers; county school board members frantically advertised nationally for new teachers to fill the classrooms of the newly constructed schools; and property owners quickly offered what had been orange groves and raw land as desirable home sites.

There were problems, of course. Longtime residents fretted about the rapid changes to Brevard County life and the disruption of the leisurely pace of events along the Indian River. Not everyone was a supporter of the space program nor the changes it brought, but gradually all the elements in the county entered into an uneasy, although profitable, arrangement. Gradually even the most reluctant Brevard Countian became a supporter of the space program and the prosperity it brought. However, being at the heart of the American space program brought other worries.

The United States was in the throes of an intense cold war with Russia, and a series of close confrontations and minor clashes kept the specter of all-out nuclear war uppermost in the minds of all Americans, especially the residents of the Space Coast. In May 1960, an American U-2, piloted by Gary Francis Powers, was shot down over the Soviet Union. Although President Dwight Eisenhower denied it, Nikita Khrushchev, the Soviet premier, produced Powers before television cameras in Moscow, along with pieces of the plane. In April 1961, President John F. Kennedy authorized the ill-fated Bay of Pigs invasion that resulted in the death or capture of 1,400 Cubans. Although the likelihood of Cuban retaliation against the United States was minimal, the relationship between the two countries came to a screeching halt and Cuba moved closer to the Soviet Union.

Tensions between Cuba, the United States, and the Soviet Union escalated again in October 1962 when American intelligence consolidated information from various sources that pointed to the construction of ICBM bases in Cuba. Although the Russian ambassador to the United States, Anatoli Dobryin, denied the existence of such facilities when questioned about the intelligence on October 13; on October 14, an American U-2 spy plane, piloted by Major Richard Heyser took almost a thousand photographs of Russian missile sites and other military installations on the island. The American response was to mobilize its land forces, to declare a naval blockade of Cuba, and to send additional airplanes, including nuclear armed B-52s, over the island. America was preparing to go to war!

For the next four weeks, the United States and Russia stood eye-to-eye and toe-to-toe in the diplomatic arena. The United States imposed a blockade of Cuba to prevent additional troops and weapons going to that island nation, while the Soviet Union was determined to maintain and expand its new outpost in North America. Events played out internationally with alarming rapidity, and radio and television newscasters were constantly interrupting "regular programming" to bring the latest developments. Armageddon seemed just seconds away.

The discovery of Soviet rockets, potentially nuclear-tipped, immediately produced a flurry of activity by the United States military, much of it conducted in secret. Nationwide, 40,000 Marines were alerted to be ready to move to the Caribbean to join the 5,000 already at Guantanamo Bay. The 82nd and 101st Airborne Divisions were designated the lead attack forces if an invasion of the Cuban mainland became necessary. In Florida, some 100,000 troops were hastily bivouacked at existing bases and the open spaces of former World War II installations. Missile batteries ringed these temporary bases and were placed strategically along open beaches. Strategic Air Command bombers were moved inland, while the latest tactical fighters took their places on the aprons of runways at bases nearer the coasts. Patrick Air Force Base, just a few miles south of the space center at Cape Canaveral, had been built as the Banana River Naval Air Station in 1939, closed, and then reopened in 1947 as the Long Range Missile Testing Base, now found its runways ringed by lumbering transports that ferried supplies for the buildup of troops. Small clusters of tents housed squads of troops from the 82nd Airborne Division, while Hawk ground-to-air missile batteries hidden in palmetto thickets and along the Atlantic beach provided air cover. F-106 Delta Darts, a supersonic all-weather fighter, rumbled along the concrete runways as they flew missions to prevent Russians bombers from making surprise raids or practiced "scrambling" to meet emergencies. Anita McClure, who lived on Merritt Island, was fourteen and recalled, "I was 14 and lived on Merritt Island. My father was just retired from the Navy and working for Pan Am. He was very interested in the incident and we talked about it frequently. I knew that the Russians had built launchers and were heading to Cuba. We had drills at school. The thing that left the most impression was that there were soldiers posted on the bridges on Cocoa Beach. Very surreal. We went to PAFB for groceries and was awestruck at the amount of air planes and tents set up for soldiers. It was a very scary time."

At first, despite the potential for espionage or sabotage, access to Patrick Air Force Base continued, and civilians were not prevented from parking on the shoulders of Highway A1A to snap photographs and to speculate on what was happening. As tensions escalated, this *laissez faire* attitude changed, and on October 18, the Cocoa *Tribune* reported that "The public was gawking at but discouraged from stopping or slowing down too much as they drove by the exposed Patrick air field where the jet plane ranks have mushroomed and their crews stand ready in their adjacent tent area." The *Tribune* continued, "Guards, some of them armed, patrol the area and, backed by newly erected 'no parking' signs, quietly discouraged staring motorists slowing down or trying to take pictures from busy Hwy. A1A which flanks the airfield on the east." Following President John F. Kennedy's speech to the nation on October 22, the military's control of the highway tightened. On October 24, the Cocoa *Tribune* once again turned to the potential problems caused by motorists seeking to see the sights at military bases. "Area Civil Defense officials and directors respectfully requested all persons to keep all driving on highways to a minimum and refrain from sightseeing at military installations."

In the same issue of the *Tribune*, Douglas Morgan Dederer, who published a weekly column, *Surfside Slant*, in the paper, wrote about the lax security, which was beginning to become more stringent, at Patrick AFB, "We drove around PAFB for about an hour-plus. The lights were on in many of the offices. The airfield bristled with red lights that seemed in greater abundance than we've ever noticed before." Dederer added, "traffic was heavy both on A1A and the base...[although] security regulations at the Cape and base have been upped perceptively, we noticed. Guards at the main gates now 'look' at the badge and face of the wearer."

Ralph Boles, who was a twelve-year old living in Eau Gallie, remembered his father taking his family to "see the sights." "Daddy took us to look at all the planes. The back road through Patrick AFB was closed to the public. Behind the big hangar next to A1A was filled with planes all the way to the Banana River. The grass areas between the taxiway and runways were covered with tents. I thought it was cool. At twelve or thirteen, I was too young to be scared." Michael Williams recalled, "My father worked at the base [and] he drove us by there. The runways had thousands of pup tents in the grassy areas. I remember seeing trains heading south loaded with tanks and trucks. Radar units were set up in the dunes along the beach."

For the latest information, residents of the Space Coast had to rely on the snowy broadcasts of the television stations in Orlando or the "rip and read" newscasts from the local radio stations like the newly established WRKT in Cocoa Beach or WEZY in Cocoa. Federal officials imposed a news blackout on military activities in Florida, but the urban nature of the various base locations prevented total secrecy. It was too difficult to mask military movements when major roads and railroads led through developed areas or when housing developments ringed military installations. Even the Titusville *Star-Advocate* noted that "Since the talk by President Kennedy [on October 22, 1962], there has been a steady stream of military loaded trains passing through Titusville on the way south." LuAnne Burgin Bettencourt, a Cocoa resident, couldn't remember her exact age at the time, but her memories of the crisis are crystal clear, "I grew up in the Pineridge development. The 800 North Fiske Apartments weren't built, and I can't really recall my exact age, but I was in elementary school. We could see the trains going by from our home, [and] they were carrying some type of weapons." Jerry Shrewsbury was also a Cocoa resident who remembered the military movements, "I never saw the missiles, but I did see the tanks and trucks heading south on the Florida East Coast railroad. I saw all the additional aircraft at Patrick Air Force Base because my mom worked at the Judge Advocate General's office at Patrick at the time, and I would visit the base with her." Nancy McIntyre Stepp was a fifteen-year-old eleventh grader at Cocoa High School at the time, but the memory of the crisis remains vivid. "I was 15 years old, in the 11th grade at CHS and lived in West Cocoa. I remember talking about it in school in American History with Colonel [Clifton] DeVoe. Also, I can remember discussions with my mom and dad and my aunt and uncle. I know they talked about my aunt and my mom driving the kids to West Virginia if something happened. My dad worked at the Cape. I remember the Rockledge Armory parking lot was loaded with big trucks. And my dad, in later years, talked about the fear and hearing that Patrick AFB was loaded with military units." Dennis Williams, a retired United States Postal Service worker, remembered, "I was a senior at Cocoa High School and working for my Dad at his service station on Highway 520 in Cocoa Beach. [I had] up close and personal views of all the military vehicles coming across the causeway. [There were] hundreds of them!" Ken Elwood was a resident of Eau Gallie (now Melbourne) in 1962 who recalled, "I remember the trains coming down the tracks in Eau Gallie loaded with lots of military equipment, and lots of semi-trucks on U. S. 1 headed to south Florida. The trains carried artillery, tanks, trucks, and Jeeps. The semi-trucks were marked with signs that said 'High Explosives.' The beach near Patrick Air Force Base had anti-aircraft batteries all up and down it."

The Cocoa *Tribune* solicited the opinions of eleventh graders in Colonel Clifton DeVoe's classes at Cocoa High School about how Cuba and Russia should be dealt with. While the 143 students, who had been given eight answers to choose from, chose different answers, the largest group (34) expressed their opinion that the United States should invoke the Monroe Doctrine and exclude Russian influence. How to do this was unanswered. Another group of thirty-one called for armed intervention by the United States and the overthrow of Fidel Castro's government, while the majority advocated the complete boycott of all trade with Cuba. Four students expressed no opinions on the matter, and a final 21 offered their own solutions to the question.

By and large, however, the three newspapers in Brevard County—the Titusville *Star-Advocate*, the Cocoa *Tribune*, and the Melbourne *Times*—maintained a united façade of "business as usual," although occasional tidbits of information about the crisis slipped out. On October 29, the editor of the *Star-Advocate* explained why the crisis impacted the Space Coast, "We have delved into the national and state matters only when these directly affected we who reside in North Brevard…We believe what happens in Cuba is of great interest to us in North Brevard. We sit only a hundred or so miles from the Red infested spot. We sit only 16 miles from the target of any Cuban or Russian attack." On October 24, the *Star-Advocate* also alerted its readers that area churches "have agreed to have their doors remain open during these critical times to permit anyone to stop, meditate, or pray." The Cocoa *Tribune* assured its readers that the "City and County Civil Defense in 'High Gear'" and that shelters, hospitals, and other emergency facilities were being prepared. Even the local Citizens' Band radio club was prepared to spring into action should the crisis move into full-scale war. The *Star-Advocate* went so far as to state, "Most veterans of World War 2…watching telecasts or listening to radio broadcasts [agreed] they'd hate to pull up and resume [their] military careers—but if that is what it would take, they'd do it."

Civil defense measures also were undertaken at local schools, although the students generally had a low opinion of the effectiveness of "duck and cover" as a defense against a nuclear attack. Gail M. Murphy recalled, "I was a third grader in Rockledge Elementary School. We lived on Hillcrest Drive in Cocoa…[and] I remember the 'talk' our teacher gave us about why we needed to practice diving under our desks." Judy Clifton Steighner added, "I remember the fear and concern as we had to practice at school in case of a missile strike. I remember us having to close all the windows in the classroom and then hiding under our desks. It was a scary time for me, as we knew my mother was fearful, so we were too." Lynn LaShure remembered, "In Indian Harbor Beach, now Martesia, my mother, a school teacher, didn't play along with the school drills much at Surfside Elementary School because she was pretty sure that an elementary school desk wasn't going to stop a missile from Cuba." Kathie Wood Howell shared LaShure's mother's opinion, "It was a very frightening time, at least for us older eighth graders—knowing full well the drills were ridiculous. Hearing SAC [Strategic Air Command] planes fly over Melbourne several times a day was little comfort." Becky Burgess Brock added this assessment on the effectiveness of "duck and cover" drills, "I was in the second grade at Rockledge Elementary School, and all I remember is the drills where we had to get under our desks and put our arms over our heads. Now I wonder just who thought that was going to help anything!"

The *Tribune* reported on October 29, that "The American Red Cross is moving its staff to bolster its services to U. S. Armed Forces while its nationwide network of chapters stands ready for any possible emergency relief action resulting from the Cuban crisis." Given the uncertainty of the outcome of the crisis, *Star-Advocate* readers were informed that "the ARC blood program has on hand an ample reserve of serum albumin—the blood component used in treatment of shock resulting from burns or other injuries. The Armed Forces also have available a large stockpile."

Local newspaper readers were also informed on October 23, that "Several hours after President Kennedy's Cuba speech, the Army launched a Pershing missile on a successful, short-range flight about 300 miles down range. It marked the first time the missile was fired from a battlefield-type, unprepared site." The Cocoa *Tribune* let its readers know that "Armed Guards Surround War Planes At Patrick," although it noted that "The only item of interest to the thousands of civil service and military personnel passing by the area was armed guards strolling about the perimeter of the [three squadrons of F-106] Air Defense Command fighters." The newspaper failed to mention the presence of two ultra-secret U-2 photo-reconnaissance planes that were stationed at Patrick AFB. Douglas Morgan Dederer also noted in his column in the *Tribune* on October 24 that although the "Signs along A1A by PAFB say 'no parking'...[the] road was lined with citizens looking at the mass of armed might contained in those F106 planes."

The newspapers' emphasis, however, remained focused on the space program at Cape Canaveral, and their editors continued to feature local news over the national emergency. On Tuesday, October 23, readers of the *Tribune* were informed that Cocoa city merchants were in favor of filling in the riverfront behind Travis Hardware and Taylor Park, and they were assured that the Cocoa High School homecoming queen would be named at half-time at the Friday night football game. On October 25, the *Tribune* reported that progress on the construction of three new buildings at the newly created Brevard Junior College was moving along at the Clearlake Road site—welcome news for the hundreds of high school graduates in the area. The same issue informed readers that the Bailey Jewelry store in downtown Cocoa had been robbed overnight of some $1,500 in watches and jewelry. The bandits made their entry through a skylight on the roof.

Still, despite the outward appearance of calm, the paper included some tidbits on how people were reacting to the missile crisis. "Central Brevard Tense," was the headline of a front-page article on the October 25 issue of the *Tribune*, "But Refuses to Panic." "An unmistakable air of tension has enveloped Central Brevard communities as a result of the Cuban crisis, but local residents, as Americans have so often in the past, apparently have decided they will not be stampeded," explained the article's author. "Most businessmen in downtown Cocoa yesterday reported business seemed to be pretty much as usual, with no particular increase or decrease in volume." The one notable exception, however, was "Jones Pharmacy on Brevard Avenue, which reported increased sales in first aid supplies. Ointments, antiseptic bandages and water purifiers were reported to be good sellers, but there apparently was no increase in sales of food concentrate or vitamins." Sales of first aid supplies might have been stimulated by advertisements that appeared in the *Star-Advocate*, the Melbourne *Times*, and the Cocoa *Tribune* that warned readers that "First Aid Supplies should be where you can get them Quick—You won't have time to go to the drug store."

The same attitude of calm appeared to be the case throughout the state, at least according to an October 25 United Press International article reprinted in the Cocoa *Tribune*. Agriculture Commissioner Doyle Conner suggested that Floridians stockpile two weeks of food, maintain a secure water reserve, and fill all car tanks with gasoline. Governor Farris Bryant urged Floridians to remain calm and to watch the film "Florida's Operation Survival." A statewide conference of school officials assembled to map out possible evacuation routes, while a school in Miami and one in Jacksonville requested that students bring blankets and fruit juice to school. Tampa gun stores reported "selling a lot of guns and ammunition and small battery radios." Precautions, the article went on, but not hysterics. However, the *Tribune* reported the same day, "There were a few individuals stocking up, such as a man yesterday who was creating his own traffic jam in trying to load nine grocery carts with canned goods, but food buying for the most part was reported normal."

Tensions escalated when Major Rudolph Anderson, Jr., flying a U-2 from McCoy Air Force Base in Orlando, was shot down and killed by a Russian missile. Anderson was the only American casualty in the crisis. The Cocoa *Tribune* quietly announced on November 1 that Anderson's body was being returned to the United States. This announcement came on the same day the *Tribune* informed its readers on November 1 that the American blockade of Cuba was firmly in place by sea and air after a brief forty-eight-hour hiatus, but the absence of on-the-spot monitors to verify that missiles were being removed caused the blockade to resume.

On November 2, newspapers along the Space Coast reported that surveillance photographs confirmed that the Soviet missile sites were being dismantled. With that, interest in the Cuban crisis seemed to die out, although an occasional article, such as the publication of a picture of LCMs (Landing Craft, medium) by Karl Hunziker briefly reignited interest. The *Tribune* reported on November 5 that the seventeen LCMs and three tugs, photographed in the Indian River Lagoon near

Rockledge, were followed "[d]uring the night [by] another wave of slightly larger numbers..." The LCMs were on their way to the Port Everglades area. The LCMs and tugs stopped for about an hour to deliver mail to Dr. Adrian Jensen, a pediatric physician and surgeon who lived in Rockledge. Why? A telephone conversation with Mrs. Jensen revealed that neither she nor the doctor knew any of the army personnel, had no connection to the military, and the "mail" that was delivered were letters from the soldiers to their families they wanted the Jensens to post for them. "They arrived at dusk," said Mrs. Jensen, "They saw an open stretch of the Indian River shore that had rocks and they decided they would practice landing their boats. Once they had landed, they walked up to our house—it was one of the few on that stretch of land—and knocked on our door. We asked them in, and for the next hour or so, they used our telephone to call home, left the letters to be mailed with us, and then departed. Later that evening, another fleet of boats came down the river. They were on their way to Port Everglades and maybe Cuba."

As Soviet technicians dismantled their rocket bases and television and newspapers published pictures of Russian ships with rockets on their decks leaving Cuba, interest in the Cuban crisis waned among residents along the Space Coast. Slowly the troop concentrations moved back to their regular bases, the portable missile and radar batteries were dismantled, and the jet fighters returned to inland bases. By November 15, little evidence of the troop and equipment buildup remained. Patrick Air Force Base returned to its normal operations.

Residents chose to concentrate on the new goal that President John F. Kennedy had articulated in his speech at Rice University on September 12, 1962—just one month before the Cuban crisis had stolen the headlines. "We choose to go to the moon," he stated. "We choose to go to the moon in this decade and do the other things, not because they are easy, but because they are hard, because that goal will serve to organize and measure the best of our energies and skills, because that challenge is one that we are willing to accept, one we are unwilling to postpone, and one which we intend to win, and the others, too." And, so, the race to the moon quickly dominated the day-to-day life of the Space Coast.

There were some lasting effects of the Cuban Missile Crisis, however. The local newspapers carried advertisements for fallout shelters, which could be built easily and cheaply. Some local residents took advantage of these offers and purchased shelters, although they were never used. Many became "party places" for teenagers, while other fell prey to the high water table in the area and filled with water—left to the ravages of rust, mold, and mildew.

Local Civil Defense officials continued to plan for another emergency, and school children continued to endure the occasional "duck and cover" drills. The Cold War was still a staple of international politics, but the crisis over Soviet missiles in Cuba became a thing of the past.

ABBREVIATED BIBLIOGRAPHY

Cocoa (Florida) *Tribune*, 1 October-20 November, 1962.

Melbourne (Florida) *Times*, 1 October-20 November, 1962.

Titusville (Florida) *Star-Advocate*, 1 October-20 November, 1962.

Solicited comments and remembrances on Facebook history sites.

- *Mosquito Beaters*
- *You Grew Up in Rockledge and Loved it*
- *You Know You Grew Up/Lived in Melbourne*
- *History and Memories of Brevard County*

CHAPTER 3

The Cuban Missile Crisis: Palm Beach County

By Janet DeVries Naughton

"My grandmother said [that] one morning we would wake up with Cuban bayonets at our throats. She was what they would today call a drama queen. One morning, I woke up to the shadow of a palm frond on the bedroom wall. I thought it was a bayonet and got very upset."

Kathryn Cavaretta

By most accounts Palm Beach County was an idyllic place to live in the early 1960s. Florida's largest county in area was named after the bounty of coconut palms planted following the 1878 wreck of *The Providencia*, a ship carrying among its cargo some 20,000 coconuts. Settlers scrambled to plant the thousands of nuts, with dreams to jumpstart a lucrative coconut industry; the result was a Tahiti-like tropical paradise.

Aside from Henry Morrison Flagler's opulent Palm Beach Royal Poinciana Hotel island resort, and Addison Mizner's Boca Raton Resort and club, most of Palm Beach County was rooted in agriculture. The original pineapple plantations were replaced with gladiola nurseries, ferneries, vegetables, mango groves, citrus, dairy and truck farms. While the earliest residents were farmers, railroad workers, teachers, shop-owners and land developers, by 1960, a booming land explosion brought constructions workers, commercial and sport fishermen, families and retirees by the thousands to coastal Palm Beach County.

When air conditioning became a common feature in new homes, and Florida's Sunshine State Parkway paved the way for smooth driving, Palm Beach County's population had burgeoned to more than 230,000 people by 1962. The county boasted modern airport terminals, a deepwater seaport for shipping, and three inlets with close proximity to the offshore Gulf Stream. Blue chip research companies were setting up shop alongside the growing bedroom communities. New industries included Pratt and Whitney's aircraft research and development center in western Palm Beach County, Minneapolis Honeywell, and Radio Corporation of America (RCA).

The Cuban Missile Crisis affected people across the county in various ways. For some people, especially former military families, the threat was something to prepare for, but not much of a worry. For many towns and cities, the crisis strained their staff and their budgets. Schools had to plan for shelters and conduct nuclear fallout drills without frightening the students. Construction companies tried to cash in on building bomb shelters. Other people just wanted to "get out of Dodge." Cuba is only 283 miles away from the center of Palm Beach County, and the looming crisis etched an indelible memory upon its citizens.

Pratt & Whitney's military and rocket engine Research and Development Center and the nearby experimental fuel plant, Air Products, Incorporated (APIX) in western Palm Beach County worried some residents. In addition to the various new housing developments springing up in the formerly sleepy little towns of Jupiter, North Palm Beach, and Palm Beach Gardens, folks were anxious about the rocket and missile weapons fuel testing and top secret U.S. Air Force missions conducted in Palm Beach County. Some accounts claim the government tried to keep the fuel testing top-secret, and created a fake fertilizer producing town called APIX, to keep the operations stealth. While the official military information was classified, and "cloaked under security regulations," *The Palm Beach Post* published several articles about APIX. An October 7, 1959 story reported that King H. Cadoo, plant operations superintendent spoke at a Rotary Club of West Palm Beach meeting to ease fears. Cadoo told about the "manufacture of liquid hydrogen, and of operations undertaken by that concern in its role of supplying various products for test programs." A November 3, 1959 *Sun-Sentinel* article reported that the APIX plant was creating "LOX," liquid hydrogen. Decades later, a retired project engineer revealed the plant experimented with "Secret Fuel One," code named Suntan, to outmaneuver Russian missiles.

A generation of Palm Beach County schoolchildren vividly remember growing up hearing about the threat of nuclear war. Few could avoid the telltale television and radio reports, newspaper accounts, or overhearing the hushed worried voices of parents discussing the impending crisis. They witnessed the seemingly endless railroad cars of armaments heading south to Key West and Cuba, helped to stockpile food, and tried to think of ways to escape the radioactive fallout or the wrath of enemy attackers.

Linda Canady recalled how her civics teacher at Conniston Middle School kept the students "informed and terrified all at the same time." The teacher held the students' attention and frightened them with "wild stories of how milk and bread would cost over a dollar, and how the Communists were going to take over." Her family didn't stockpile food or supplies, but she clearly remembered feeling "sick and scared, but nothing else." Aside from the enlightening lessons from the Civics teacher, most adults kept the children sheltered from "serious issues."

Victor Archambeau was an eight-year-old student attending South Olive Elementary School. He lived on Gregory Road near the Lake Worth Canal in the south end of West Palm Beach. He recalled one night at the dinner table his parents had a serious discussion regarding the convoys and bombers flying overhead, and the graveness of the situation. The man across the street had purchased materials to build a bomb shelter, but after realizing the water table was so close to the surface, an underground shelter was not possible. His father wanted to send him, his mother, and brother to New Hampshire to stay with relatives to be out-of-range of the missiles. His mother objected saying, "No, we are a family, and we will either live together or die together, but we will stay together."

Bill Craven, a twelve-year-old living in Whispering Pines in Lake Worth and a Sacred Heart Academy student, came up with a plan "to take my .22 single shot rifle and hide out in the Everglades when the Russians invaded from Cuba." The brave youngster thought that he'd "live off the land, with no real experience except for shooting black birds at the Schmitt Pony Ranch west of Lantana." In retrospect, he admits that "I would have ended up as gator bait."

Kathryn Cavaretta was a six-year-old first grader attending Belvedere Elementary School during the Crisis. She remembers seeing troops in camouflage riding in army vehicles down Military Trail and being terrified because of some of the things the adults said. "My grandmother said [that] one morning we would wake up with Cuban bayonets at our throats. She was what they would today call a drama queen. One morning, I woke up to the shadow of a palm frond on the bedroom wall. I thought it was a bayonet and got very upset."

Brad Williams was ten years old and lived due east of the airport [Palm Beach International]. He recalled seeing and hearing the big bomber planes flying in and out. Julie Clarkson was nine years old and living in Lake Clarke Shores. She heard what was going on from the news but confessed that "to see all those huge planes carrying bombs was really frightening." Everyone was relieved when Khrushchev changed his mind but felt "it was too close for comfort." Clarkson recalled that the "bomb shelter signs were in our schools by the front office and sporadically around the school and by custodial offices. They were also in stores like Burdines."

The Palm Beach County Board of Education instituted procedural emergency drills at all schools. The idea was that if the sirens were activated, faculty and administrators were to facilitate students in seeking cover by instructing them to lay, sit or crouch on the floor and cover their heads. If there were enough time, students were ushered to a public shelter.

Even 55 years after the ominous events, Colleen Shaffer (then Colleen Corie) still vividly remembers the Cuban Missile Crisis and the standard school "Duck-and-Cover" air raid drills. She attended the newly constructed rural Greenacres Elementary School located in the center of rapidly growing Palm Beach County. As she remembers, a shiny silver loudspeaker with dozens of small holes was centered above the blackboard. A familiar voice (likely the school's principal or vice principal) calmly alerted students and teachers to take cover. Obediently and efficiently, the students crouched down and took cover under their desks. The drills lasted but minutes, yet were firmly engrained in the memories of the youngsters who dutifully stopped mid-lesson to follow safety protocols issued by the Civil Defense Council and executed by the Palm Beach County Board of Instruction.

Greenacres (named Greenacres City at that time) was a small township on former farmland located in western Lake Worth. Edward Eissey, the popular administrator who later served as president of the then Palm Beach Junior College, was school principal. Shaffer recalls her family watching news reports of the crisis on one of the three television stations available on their black and white television. "At the time we had ABC, CBS, and NBC. Our family had a very large roof antenna, and could pick up the signal fairly clearly. If you lived just outside the city limits as we did, it was considered the boondocks. Some elderly neighbors in the area had makeshift antennae created with the aid of tin foil."

A Palm Beach County native, Ginger L. Pedersen, grew up hearing the unbelievable story of how her mother, father, older sister and grand-parents fled to Australia during the Cuban Missile Crisis threat. Her father, Jack Pedersen and grandfather, John Pedersen, founded and operated Africa U.S.A, a Boca Raton tourist attraction. The popular animal theme park, located on 300 acres near U.S. 1, operated from 1953 to 1961 and superseded Walt Disney Land on the cover of *Life* magazine in 1961. A combination of urban sprawl and escalating land prices as well as increasing government regulations on animal parks and public safety closed the animal theme park.

Pedersen and son, already avid real estate investors, built a small num-ber of custom homes. Deepening concern over the threat of the atomic bomb and Palm Beach County's close proximity to Cuba inspired Pedersen to sell his dream house and vacate quickly. Jack Pedersen decided to take his family to Australia, as he was convinced that locale was safe from radioactive fallout. Pedersen took out a full page in the April 1962, *Palm Beach Post* announcing that the family was "Going to Australia: So our one-year-old lakefront home will be sold far below cost." Pedersen offered his Town of Lake Clarke Shores custom built, 3,200 square foot Colonial style home, all of its furnishings, his 14-foot boat with a 22-horsepower motor and full value title insurance policy – for $43,500 – far below cost. The three-bedroom, two-bath house surrounded by a wide green lawn with yellow hibiscus and an 18-foot by 40-foot in-ground pool located less than three miles from the Atlantic Ocean sold quickly.

Pedersen, his wife Christa, and one-year-old daughter Barbara, along with his parents, John and Lillian drove to California and sailed to Surfer's Paradise, Australia. They took their car and a few trunks of clothing, and not much else. Their Australian adventure lasted a little more than a year; when it looked as if the Cuban Missile Crisis was truly over, the family sailed back to the United States.

The most notorious nuclear bomb fallout shelter in Palm Beach County was built in 1961 at a cost of $97,000 for the newly inaugurated President John Fitzgerald Kennedy. At that time, the Kennedy family's vacation compound in Palm Beach, at 1095 N. Ocean Blvd., was known as "The Winter White House" and several generations of Kennedy's, including JFK and family spent vacations and weekends there. The rambling 11-bedroom Mediterranean-style home designed by famed architect Addison Mizner, faced the Atlantic Ocean and boasted 200 feet of beachfront. A number of sites on the island of Palm Beach were considered possible locations, however the island was too small to enable construction of the top-secret bunker.

Navy Seabees constructed a 1,600-square foot underground bunker in just ten days on nearby Hood's Island (now Peanut Island), behind the Coast Guard Station. The bunker, with room enough for Kennedy, 30 members of his family, aides and military advisors is accessible via a 40-foot corrugated steel tunnel. Buried under 12 feet of dirt and 18 inches of concrete, the shelter was designed with 12-foot ceilings and a cement floor.

There are conflicting reports if Kennedy ever saw the bunker before his 1963 assassination. Official documents described the locale as a "Detachment Hotel," and the government didn't formally acknowledge its existence until 1974. The secret fallout shelter, code named "Hotel," was a ten-minute boat ride from the President's Palm Beach retreat. The complex was stocked with government supplies including dehydrated food was and said to be self-sufficient for 30 days. The structure included air filtering equipment, a decontamination room, chemical toilets, a diesel generator, and two emergency exits. According to tour guides at the Palm Beach Maritime Museum, some young boys exploring the island in the early 1970s stumbled upon the hatch leading to the presidential bunker, climbed down and shared the discovery with their parents. The museum restored the mostly forgotten island bunker and opened it for public display in 1998.

The John F. Kennedy Bunker tourist attraction, accessible only by boat, is equipped with two of the 15 sets of metal bunk beds, a "communication station" including a ham radio, three telephones, two black and one the famous "red" phone. There is a replica of a wooden desk where the president would have worked, an ashtray, and a world globe. Barrels that would have served as toilets and an array of military rations remind the 12,000 people who visit the atomic age bunker annually of the graveness of the situation in October 1962.

Local Civil defense authorities took an aggressive stance as the likelihood of nuclear war increased. Fallout shelters were installed in most government facilities. In the 1960s, there was a model fallout shelter on the lawn of the Palm Beach County Courthouse along Dixie Highway. The Wonderbuilt Living Fallout Shelter and equipment was on display at the entrance to the Grandview Heights neighborhood at 1603 S. Dixie Highway, West Palm Beach. In Lake Park, the new First Federal Savings & Loan Association had the foresight to build their new banking facility to be equipped as a Civil Defense shelter with space designated as a fallout shelter.

In March of 1961, the Office of Civil Defense Mobilization opened a prototype above ground family demonstration shelter in Golfview at 21 Gun Club Road. Constructed by the Overland Construction Company, the shelter was specifically designed to protect up to six people from "radiation effects of an atomic raid." The demonstration shelter was equipped with and array of survival items including fold up cots, blankets, sanitary supplies, a transistor radio and enough food and water for three days. Colonel Ellis F. Altman described the structure's unique construction as:

> The walls of the shelter are 20 inches thick, consisting of two eight-inch blocks and one four-inch and one four-inch block of the heavy-weight type. Spaces in the blocks are filled with mortar and the blocks are tied together with steel. The roof is a six-inch slab of reinforced concrete, with 20 inches of pit run gravel till, with water-proofed asphalt surfacing on this fill. Air intake and exhaust pipes are three inches in diameter, with filter caps and a hand cranked blower on the intake pipe.

Palm Beach County Plans and Operations Coordinator/Civil Defense Director Major A.L. Fullerton and his wife built a 10 by 12-foot fallout shelter at their Lake Park home. The Fullertons stocked the shelter with food and water, a first-aid kit, radio and batteries, a slide projector and slides, books and games. The shelter had room enough for six adults and closed with a 450-pound lead door. In an April 21, 1967 *Palm Beach Post* interview, Fullerton asserted that there were some 200 family-fall-out shelters in Palm Beach County.

Private citizens executed their own shelter plans. E. A. Burdick, who owned a home at 711 Nathan Hale Road, West Palm Beach, constructed a fallout shelter on his property for $800. Burdick filled his bunker, which was topped with a strong five-foot thick roof, with $700 in supplies. Chuck Young, local Civil Defense instructor, was on hand for the July 17, 1961 unveiling.

Civil Defense directors reported that there were more fallout shelters constructed in the two weeks of the "October Crisis" than in the entire previous two years' period. Many of the shelters were substandard and haphazardly built because the cost of professionally constructed shelters with blowers for ventilation and radiological meters to check radioactive levels was prohibitive for most people. The average cost of a professionally build small shelter was around $1,500, more than double the cost of a home built unit.

According to Palm Beach County Archaeologist Christian Davenport, "The majority of the cold war's activities were clandestine. Palm Beach County's role in the cold war remains shrouded today." Davenport explained that given the shallow water table and slab on grade construction methods used here most people could not have built a bomb shelter even if they wanted to. Davenport asserted "Evidence of the impact on the area is only witnessed by a few personal bomb shelters built in luxury homes and forgotten bomb shelters in the backyards of a few modest homes along the coastal dune and ridge system."

As the threat of nuclear war loomed closer, during the September 25, 1961 Delray Beach City council meeting, City Clerk Robert D. Worthing read Resolution No. 1350 directing the city tax assessor to assess qualified fall-out shelters at rates comparable to the present assessment basis used for garages, carports and open porches. The council unanimously adopted the resolution.

The City of Delray Beach then passed a Resolution adopting an Operational Survival Plan and creating an organizational chart for Civil Defense at a Special Meeting on November 12, 1962. The City's plan was based upon the January 1, 1962 plan created by Palm Beach County in conformity with the Statutes of the State of Florida and the National Plan for Civil Defense and Defense Mobilization.

At the same meeting, City Clerk Worthing read a Resolution to provide, in the event of attack upon the United States, for the continuity of the executive functions of the government of the City of Delray Beach, Palm Beach County, State of Florida, by the designation of additional officials to serve for the duly elected or appointed officials of the City of Delray Beach, Palm Beach County when such elected or appointed officials are unavailable.

The Town of Jupiter enacted similar proclamations and activities. George H. Butler, mayor, was appointed director of the Jupiter Civil Defense Council. Mayor Butler claimed that forming a local Civil Defense Council would allow the Town to purchase trucks, radios and emergency supplies at low prices. The Town Council discussed fall-out shelter standards at several meetings. They decided to leave approval up to the building inspectors until government standards were issued.

Palm Beach County and its various municipalities reacted to the escalating conflict by designating and equipping public shelters, readying its medical facilities, and establishing a formal chain of command. As the seriousness of the crisis deepened, Congressman Paul Rogers pushed to designate Palm Beach International Airport as a recovery area. The airport also ordered spectators away from the airport, as so many people were showing up to gawk at the large bomber planes and supply planes.

The September 7, 1962 *Palm Beach Post* reported that National Civil Defense and State Board of Health representatives had visited the county to determine if medical facilities were equipped to "become operative in case of natural or nuclear disaster." Civil Defense Director Colonel Ellis F. Altman declared that the team of representatives "found Palm Beach County's 200–bed emergency hospital in tip-top shape." In the same article Altman announced that "bids for construction of a Palm Beach County Civil Defense emergency center will be advertised...received September 24." The new center located on Belvedere Road would serve as headquarters for Civil Defense and the Sheriff's department as well as an alternate location for the county commission in the event of nuclear disaster.

"Stay Calm, Cool, County CD Chief Advises" declared the main headline in the morning edition of the October 25, 1962, *Palm Beach Post.* "Don't go haywire," warned Colonel Altman. The Civil Defense Director claimed his office had been bombarded with calls from county residents asking for advice. "We are not anticipating any nuclear attack, but we must be ready," counseled the Colonel, a WWI and WWII veteran. Altman claimed that he would "rather be in Florida than as any other place in the United States" during this crisis, explaining that large cities and industrial meccas were on the radar for enemy missiles rather than the then mostly rural Palm Beach County. Altman advised that residents stay where they were and gather supplies such as battery-operated flashlights and radios, first-aid kits, non-perishable food and drinking water, etc. The list may sound much like preparing for an Atlantic hurricane or other natural disaster, until one reads past the requisite food, water and paper plates:

> 14-day supply of food...cooking and eating utensils, matches, garbage and waste disposal cans, personal sanitary supplies, blankets, disinfectants, wrench, screwdriver and shovel, axe and crowbar to free self from debris.

The article closed by reiterating that residents should listen to the radio for alerts, and that the county had an adequate supply of radiation detectors for use by trained Civil Defense personnel.

The next day, October 26, 1962, local response to the intense Cuban situation was buried on page 13 of the *Palm Beach Post*. The largest headline reported that there was no noted panic buying or stock-piling in Palm Beach County. W. P. Moffitt, head of the Merchant Division of the Greater West Palm Beach/Palm Beach County Chamber of Commerce insisted that the short uptick in buying in October came as a result of seasonal visitors. On the same page, *The Post* reported that Leonard Fairman, Riviera Beach's Civil Defense head pronounced that the City of Riviera Beach has "one of the best Civil Defense set-ups in Palm Beach County." Riviera is well prepared with two rescue vehicles with generators, 100 cots for casualties, 48 workers trained in first aid and civil defense, as well as "radiological detection apparatus and a Civil Defense office and storage building on Port Road."

An adjacent report cited Major A. L. Fullerton Assistant Civil Defense Director claiming that Bethesda Hospital, the approved shelter for the Lake Worth area, refused to sign papers and was no longer available as a shelter. The City of Boynton had reported in the prior year that the new Bethesda Hospital on Seacrest Blvd. had space for 106 people in case of nuclear disaster. According to hospital administrator, Dr. Merrill Steele, "The hospital needed all of the space for their patients and staff members in the event of an attack, and although the shelter is supplied, there are no facilities for any of the public." Colonel Altman advised that the county was still waiting on supplies for its other 16 public shelters. Major Fullerton explained that the county was not allowed to purchase shelter supplies on the open market, as all food and materials for the shelters must come legally through the federal government.

Democratic Senator George Smathers also tried to quell fear among Florida citizens. *The Post* reported that Senator Smathers addressed guests at a coffee held in his honor at the Delray Beach Country Club via special telephone hook-up with Washington and insisted that "Florida is not in any greater danger than any other area of the nation." Smathers claimed that the Cuban missiles were geared for distances much further away than nearby Palm Beach County, making it an unlikely target. He told the group, "Since the President made it clear that an attack by Cuba will be considered to be an attack by the Soviet Union, it is at least safer that over-emotional Cubans are not manning the missile launchers. The Russians are apparently as worried as we are by the prospect of an accidental war."

Palm Beach County officials continued their struggle to find adequate fallout shelters for its residents. A November 1, 1962, *Palm Beach Post* article noted that although 56 private owners offered their buildings for private use, those buildings were not deemed safe enough by government standards. Public shelter designation also specified a minimum of 50 people, hence many of the buildings were turned down. Major A.L. Fullerton, assistant director of public defense announced plans for a stepped-up fallout shelter plan that would ease requirement and increase space from 2,660 to 34,945 people. The November 28, 1962 edition of the same newspaper published an article announcing that the U.S. Army Corps of Engineers had approved 11 buildings in Palm Beach County as public fallout shelters. The article claimed that people in the shelters would be 40 times safer than "outdoors during a nuclear attack." The 11 shelters could house 4,206 people and would be "stocked with food, water and medical supplies at the government's expense." The paper listed the names and locations of the 11 shelters and their capacity and Colonel Altman assured readers that additional shelters meeting requirements had been identified, and would be announced once the owners cleared the facilities for public use.

> Juno, Seminole Golf Clubhouse, 130; Lake Park, First Federal Savings and Loan Assn., 56; Palm Beach, Monte Cristo Hotel, 228; West Palm Beach, La Fontana Co-operative Apartments, 1,161; Northwood Baptist Church and school, 124; Harvey Building, 509; Palm Beach County Court House, 216; Town House Motor Hotel, 1,265; Citizens Building, 332; Florida National Bank, 130; Atlantic National Bank, 55.

Local municipalities, in line with Palm Beach County Civil Defense, formulated their local response to nuclear fallout and budgets and manpower were stretched. The City of Boynton Beach Fire Chief, John "Jack" Tuite also served as the city's Civil Defense Director. Tuite used large, hand-written flow charts to identify the chain of command in case of a nuclear attack or other emergency. From the top down the plan listed the Mayor, Civil Defense Council (consisting of the Town Council), Civil Defense Director and the Assistant Civil Defense Director. Tuite outlined five distinct areas of responsibility within the city: Warning (Fire Dept. and Communications); Shelters (Building Official, Survey, Manning, and Emergency Food); Public Health (Medical Staff, Public Water and Medical Supplies); Public Safety (Police – Traffic; Security, Mob Control, Damage Survey; Intelligence) and

(Fire Department – Fire Defense; Rescue, First Aid, Decontamination, Underwater Search and Rescue) and Public Works Department (Maintenance, Roads, Transportation; Control Fuel Supplies and Food Supplies, and Control Evacuation Area). The City of Boynton Beach also budgeted for an air-raid alarm siren, even though some other cities, such as Riviera Beach, claimed that they would not sound their alarm because to do so would cause widespread panic.

The Lake Park Town Commission established the Town of Lake Park Civil Defense Council comprised on the members of the Mayor and Town Commissioners on June 19, 1961. Civil Defense budgets for local municipalities doubled from 1961 to 1962 as towns scrambled to plan for fallout from nuclear disaster. The Town of Lake Park's civil defense budget rose from $500 in 1961 to $1,000 in 1962.

The small municipality also formally adopted its Operational Survival Plan in the form of Resolution No. 302 citing "The political, economic, and cultural aspirations of the world powers are at hostile variance." Palm Beach County Civil Defense Director Major A. L. Fullerton headed the Lake Park Council and was responsible for the seven-page plan "compiled to assist Town Officials in that structure to combat the effects of disaster." The plan was simpler than most, with just four categories of service—Public Safety, Social Services, Logistical Services and Administrative Services. Sub-categories included police, fire and rescue, communications, intelligence, radiological, medical, welfare, religious, mortuary, engineering, transportation, supply, records, registration, manpower, fiscal, training, education, and resources management. In the midst of the Cuban Missile Crisis, on October 29, 1962, Major Fullerton resigned as head of the Lake Park Civil Defense Council due to his obligations with Palm Beach County Civil Defense.

According to November 8, 1962 Palm Beach County School Board minutes, to further prepare the community for the crisis, the School Board started offering Civil Defense classes through the Adult Veteran

Section of the school system. The classes were offered in areas where people indicated an avid interest. While the courses were not a part of the formal County Civil Defense Program, the work was closely allied as County Civil Defense Director Colonel Ellis Altman and Dugal G. Campbell collaborated in this regard. Campbell expressed hope that Tallahassee would release a greater number of classes in the future. The Superintendent reported Colonel Altman has had requests for the present *Program of Evacuation* for the schools and several other counties had adopted the plan.

The Palm Beach County School Board improved its emergency communication system by installing intercoms in classrooms. In December 1962, Flamingo Electronics was awarded a $1,874.00 contract for "Installation of Intercommunications" at East Lake High School and Flamingo Electronics installed intercoms at Roosevelt Elementary. The telecommunications system was soon added to North Palm Beach Elementary, Riviera Beach High and Lincoln High by Techni-Services of West Palm Beach. The school also granted the use of schools as Medical Aid Stations for Civil Defense Emergencies in 1963.

As time went on, life began to normalize. Teenagers used the battery powered transistor radios purchased for emergencies to listen to top-forty hit-music poolside on am stations like WHEW 1660 and WIRK 1290. Shelters built for protection from atomic bomb fallout became musty storage rooms for old golf clubs and holiday decorations. Memories of the Cuban Missile Crisis in Palm Beach County have gradually disappeared for most of its residents. The composition of the community rapidly changed and grew in the next decade. By the mid-1970s, the signature shell shops with the alligator purses and roadside fruit stands with the "all you can drink" grapefruit juice for ten cents faded like snapshots in an old family photo album. Undeveloped land has turned into cookie cutter housing developments and high rise condominiums. Generations of permanent residents and seasonal visitors have experienced both the beauty, and the vulnerability of our open shoreline.

ACKNOWLEDGEMENTS

Chris Davenport, Shaquita Edwards, Shayla Ellis, Desiree Estabrook, Sue Gillis, Nick Golubov, Glendia Harvey, Michael Landress, Suvi Morales, Friederike Mittner, Michael P. Naughton, Chevelle Nubin, Elizabeth Ojea, Ginger L. Pedersen, Gretel Sarmiento, and Mary Pinkerman.

CHAPTER 4

The Cuban Missile Crisis:
The Suncoast and Tampa Bay Region

BY JAMES ANTHONY SCHNUR

"Folks are staying put, visitors are arriving daily, there is no panic buying and it's been business as usual."

Clearwater Sun, October 26, 1962

Located along the central west coast of Florida, the Tampa Bay region has had a close relationship with Cuba since conquistadors first came to the area in the sixteenth century. During the 1700s and 1800s, small itinerant Cuban fishing rancheros appeared along the coastline from the Pinellas peninsula southward. Cubans fished the rich waters of the Gulf of Mexico, bays and estuaries, and rivers, smoking their abundant catches to preserve them before returning to Cuba. Long before Cubans came to the Miami area in great numbers beginning in the 1950s, the Tampa Bay region attracted Cuban cigar workers who first arrived at settlements such as Ybor City and West Tampa in Hillsborough County in the 1880s. Rough Riders under the leadership of Colonel Theodore Roosevelt prepared for the invasion and liberation of Cuba from their camps at Tampa during the Spanish-American War in 1898. Tampa's close connections with Cuba began before Miami existed as a municipality.

The Tampa Bay region rapidly urbanized in the years following the Second World War. Although retirees continued to make up a large proportion of seasonal visitors, many newcomers hailed from the Midwest, Pennsylvania, New York, and New England. Some of these transplants first visited Florida while training at one of the nearly 175 military installations that operated in the Sunshine State during World War II; others arrived to work in the plants operated by General Electric, Honeywell, Sperry Microwave Electronics, and other businesses with federal contracts. Although agricultural harvests remained an important component within the local economy, the rapid development of new residential subdivisions, businesses, and transportation corridors redefined the area. By 1960, industries related to the Cold War and military operations played an important role in the financial wellbeing of the region.

The military maintained a strong presence, even if the number of installations declined. The Pinellas Army Airfield and Drew Field transformed from military to civilian control, as these installations became St. Petersburg-Clearwater International Airport and Tampa International Airport, respectively. Much of the former Henderson Air Field, an auxiliary site north of Tampa, became the campus of the University of South Florida after the legislature and board of regents established the school in 1956. The former United States Maritime Service Training Station along Bayboro Harbor south of downtown St. Petersburg had new life as the interim campus of Florida Presbyterian (now Eckerd) College. MacDill Air Force Base along the Interbay Peninsula between Tampa Bay and Hillsborough Bay remained in operation. Originally known as Southeast Field when established in 1939, the base was renamed in honor of Lieutenant Colonel Leslie MacDill. The base served as a home for

Strategic Air Command (SAC) during the 1950s but faced an uncertain fate on the eve of President John F. Kennedy's inauguration. In December 1960, military leaders talked about closing MacDill by 1962 and using part of the site as a veterans' hospital. However, as tensions mounted in Cuba, the U.S. Strike Command deployed at MacDill in 1961. Mobilization at MacDill began prior to the Cuban Missile Crisis of October 16-28, 1962. If anything, this international crisis elevated the importance of the base and kept it in operation.

Fidel Castro's consolidation of power in the late 1950s and Fulgencio Batista's downfall on January 1, 1959 had an immediate impact on the long-established Cuban American communities along the Suncoast. When local Cubans learned of Castro's victory, they had mixed reactions. Celebrations occurred as those in Ybor City learned of Batista's demise. Many Latinos remembered when Fidel Castro had visited Ybor City in November 1955 with hopes of raising funds to overthrow Batista. Although Castro could not get the Cuban Club or Italian Club to rent him space for a public event, Tampa historian Tony Pizzo remembered that Castro held a gathering at a labor union meeting hall on November 27, 1955 with more than 300 in attendance and offered interviews about his plans to a local television and radio station. Before departing, Castro also established a Tampa branch of his 26th of July Movement, a revolutionary group that he led in his attempt to overthrow Batista's regime. Although Castro failed to raise large sums during his Tampa visit, he did receive support for his cause during his brief stop in the area. He also had a chance to see places that Cuban revolutionary and patriot José Martí had visited more than sixty years earlier, including the Vicente Martinez-Ybor Cigar Factory.

During the mid-1950s, Castro understood the important role that Tampa had played in an earlier movement for Cuban independence. Observers might assume that the Cuban communities of Ybor City and West Tampa would have expressed outrage over Castro's ascent, especially given the cries of "Cuba libre!" heard in these settlements that had developed well-established Cuban immigrant populations since the 1880s. Indeed, both Ybor City—a company town established by Vicente Martinez-Ybor in the mid-1880s with help of the Tampa Board of Trade—and West Tampa—a separate municipality between 1895 and 1925—attracted many Cuban immigrants between the 1880s and 1920s who had a strong sense of nationalism. The earliest waves supported or participated in the move for independence led and inspired by José Martí before his death in 1895 and gained through campaigns during the Spanish American War in 1898. Although some conservative Cuban Americans in Hillsborough County expressed concern with Castro's alliance with Russia, many residents had little love of Fulgencio Batista's dictatorship that had received strong backing of the United States due to his professed hatred of Communism and his corrupt partnerships with American mob and corporate interests.

Unlike the exiles arriving in the Keys, Miami, and other locations along southeastern Florida who fled from Castro's regime, the majority of residents in older and more established Cuban communities in the Tampa Bay area did not view Castro one-dimensionally within the framework of the Cold War, at least initially. José Yglesias, a 1919 native of Ybor City and novelist who often wrote about revolutions, often reminded readers in his writings about his hometown that Ybor was a "radical, trade union town," a place where mutual aid societies offered socialized medicine and other security nets that outsiders (whom he called "*americanos*") often viewed as Communist-inspired. During the height of the cigar industry before the 1930s, the workers hired the readers (*los lectores*) in the factories and that the *lector* in many factories regularly read both anarchist newspapers (before the First World War) and Communist newspapers such as the New York *Daily Worker* (after Bolsheviks gained control in Russia) along with literary works well into the 1930s. In a community where throngs of cigar workers would strike and shut down factories when managers tried to remove *los lectores*, Ybor City became, according to Yglesias, a "radical island in the [American] South" before World War II.

Although revolutionary impulses moderated after the Second World War, fervent anticommunism did not grip many of the older Cuban Americans in the Tampa Bay region as profoundly as in the exile communities in southern Florida. Mechanization of the factories, migration of younger generations outside of Tampa's Latin Quarters, and the Cuban trade embargo had strong effects on the demise of the Cigar City's most noted industry. However, Yglesias reminded outsiders in his writings that many Cubans in Ybor City were *fidelistas* even after 1959. Old generations remembered that *americano* "crackers" had often used intimidation, worked with the Ku Klux Klan, and attacked them at their union meetings for decades, and a sense of mistrust persisted between Anglos and Latinos in Tampa. To some of the elderly Cubans in Tampa who came to Ybor City and West Tampa as young revolutionaries, newer Cuban counterrevolutionary exiles were as "untrustworthy" as the *americanos*.

Castro understood this dichotomy. According to a retrospective article in the November 27, 2015 of the *Tampa Tribune* that commemorated the sixtieth anniversary of Castro's Tampa speech, Castro told Tampans in November 1955 that he hoped to return to the Cigar City one day to thank residents for supporting his revolution. A few leaders of Tampa's 26th of July Movement soon traveled to Cuba to meet with Castro. Others sent cash, medicine, clothes, various supplies, and even weapons in support of Castro before and after the embargo took effect in 1961. Other members of Tampa's Cuban community, however, ended their support for Castro long before 1959, seeing any regime change in Cuba as a possible threat to the United States.

Tampa's long-established Cuban communities had also witnessed the shift in Cubans' interest as a preferred tourist destination from the Tampa Bay region to Miami and south Florida a decade before Castro took control and exiles flooded those areas *en masse*. As historian Tony Pizzo remembered, by that late 1940s, regular passenger boats between Havana and Tampa had declined, while new routes took enthusiastic summertime vacationers from Havana to Miami and Miami Beach. While older Cubans remembered Tampa as "the cradle of Cuban Liberty," younger generations preferred the beaches of Miami-Dade County at about the same time that the children and grandchildren of Tampa's Latino community began to abandon Ybor and West Tampa for new Suncoast subdivisions where Latinos had once been denied entry. By the early 1960s, urban renewal programs and the bisecting of both Ybor City and West Tampa by interstate highways had forced the dispersal of most Cuban Americans to new neighborhoods. The strengthening of the Cuban embargo with President Kennedy's executive order in February 1962 dealt a fatal blow to Tampa's once vibrant cigar industry. No longer able to secure the preferred tobacco leaves from Cuba, the thirty-five remaining factories and their 6,000 employees knew the industry would soon be up in smoke.

Military and humanitarian operations transformed Florida's relationship with Cuba as the embargo tightened and Castro strengthened his alliance with the Soviet Union. As a retrospective article on the seventy-fifth anniversary of MacDill mentioned in the 16 April 2016 edition of the *Tampa Tribune,* American planes based out of Guantanamo Bay had carefully taken aerial images above Cuba as concerns about Russian influence increased. MacDill played an important role in American spy operations as this surveillance film photographed over the island by soldiers in Guantanamo-based aircraft made its way to MacDill, where technicians usually developed it before relaying the images to officials at the Pentagon. Throughout 1962, new deployments of enlisted men, officers, and technicians overwhelmed the base as many of them occupied former barracks used previously during World War II as well as hotels in downtown Tampa. Also, between December 1960 and October 1962, Operation Peter Pan (Operación Pedro Pan) brought approximately 14,000 children and teenagers from Cuba to Florida, primarily Miami, as Castro's powerbase began to align with the Soviet Union. Although many of these new arrivals remained in southern Florida, some relocated to the Tampa Bay region.

As tensions escalated in mid-1962, residents of Pinellas County on the western side of Tampa Bay engaged in a different series of wartime battles. Between July 24 and September 28, much of the county fell under a major epidemic of St. Louis encephalitis that killed at least thirty-eight people and led to much suffering and concern from this mosquito-borne illness. Since the elderly had the greatest chance of succumbing and the areas around St. Petersburg catered to many retirees, officials launched an all-out war against mosquitoes and targeted areas with standing water. In his research on this epidemic, historian Eric Jarvis noted that local public health officials employed warlike rhetoric to describe the eradication campaign. The State Board of Health called infected mosquitoes "man's greatest enemy" that required "night and day battle" to defeat. Authorities also engaged in a "war on local birds," according to *The Nation*.

This military mindset to a public health threat covered the pages of the *St. Petersburg Times* in August and September 1962. Hoping to fight this menace "with every weapon at our disposal," an August 29 editorial informed readers that battalions of pest control workers needed a "big war chest to open an immediate sustained offensive against mosquitoes." In some communities, such as Dunedin, teams of Civil Defense workers canvassed neighborhoods on a block-by-block basis to quarantine and obliterate the enemy. While distributing more than 100,000 booklets to residents, St. Petersburg's Council of Neighborhood Associations called upon citizens to volunteer in a protracted battle to locate and clean areas susceptible to mosquitoes. After St. Petersburg's city council passed an ordinance that outlawed the feeding of wild birds—a popular practice by many senior citizens in parks—fears escalated that police might arrest elderly residents for giving bread crumbs to "Public Enemy #1." Crews contained ducks, swans, pigeons, and many other birds, including peacocks, as prisoners of war, killing any that appeared sick.

Although these maneuvers against mosquitoes and battles against birds seem far removed from the serious crisis fomenting in Cuba as Castro aligned his nation with the Soviets, they reflected the prevalence of the militaristic, almost jingoistic narratives within the press and public discourse that defined battles against any perceived "enemy" at the same that Cold War fears gripped the Suncoast. As news reports of tensions in Cuba and in Europe—especially between East and West Berlin with the newly constructed Berlin Wall in place—filled the airwaves in the Tampa Bay region, concerns of containing any other perceived threat grew during mid- and late 1962. Local encephalitis patrols stepped up their efforts: Seventeen fogging trucks covered Pinellas County, exterminating mosquitoes with clouds of malathion and diesel fuel that created clouds in the sky, while corps of citizen volunteers used DDT along porches and poured kerosene or other oils into pools of standing water. Jarvis noted that irony that this full-blown war that damaged the local environment took place just as Rachel Carson, a visitor to the Tampa Bay region in the 1950s, released her landmark publication, *Silent Spring.* This book, released in September 1962, condemned the widespread use of pesticides as a threat to the environment. Fearing that ongoing media coverage of the encephalitis scare might harm the upcoming tourist season, local officials decided a war against the environment was a small price to pay.

Concerns about encephalitis in the Tampa Bay region disappeared as tensions grew between the United States and Cuba. Indeed, the arrival of cooler fall temperatures, the demise of mosquitoes, and the disappearance of local and national news stories about St. Louis encephalitis allowed chambers of commerce in the Tampa Bay region to focus on the upcoming arrival of snowbirds. As tensions grew in mid-October, newspapers in St. Petersburg initially focused on local matters and sought to boost tourism in the Sunshine City during the upcoming winter season. The front page of the October 16 edition of the *St. Petersburg Times* included a caption below a large picture proclaiming that "On The Smiling Suncoast—Every Day's a Holiday!" That day, the *Times* ran its popular "Suncoast Holiday Edition" that also included a large number of reprints for locals to send to their snowbird friends. The October 17 edition of St. Petersburg's afternoon paper, the *Evening Independent*, noted that one of the biggest agenda items the city council planned to consider was whether community leaders and businesses could once again paint the city's fabled benches an olive-green color. A year earlier, in a move to rejuvenate the city's image as a retirement haven, leaders approved the Project '61 initiative that called for the removal of the green color from the palette as a way of creating a more youthful image. Such discussion soon seemed trivial as conditions along the Straits of Florida deteriorated. One letter writer on October 29 in the *Times* lambasted St. Petersburg's Civil Defense plans, ones that called for some department stores to serve as shelters and that did not seem as coordinated as what was found in other municipalities. The writer claimed that instead of thinking about appropriate shelters with adequate provisions, "this city is busy with such nonsensical hobbies as painting the benches green to please the old people."

The larger issue (and dominating headline) of the October 17 *St. Petersburg Times* was growing concern of American involvement in Vietnam and potential stormy weather from Tropical Storm Ella, an erratic low-pressure system in the Atlantic that passed through the Bahamas. A "No 'Deal' on Cuba" editorial by the *Times* on October 17 emphasized the importance of containing any totalitarian threat, but also placed part of the blame for escalating tensions on bellicose members of Congress who failed to recognize "that the Monroe Doctrine went out of date years ago."

As Ella became a full hurricane and turned towards the Carolinas, heads turned toward the headlines on October 18 as military authorities strengthened air defenses at MacDill in response to the Soviet presence in Cuba. Airplanes arrived and training exercises expanded at MacDill as pilots flew many planes in the Tactical Air Command (TAC) fleet to MacDill on October 17. Sirens blared onsite throughout the day, beginning at 2:00 a.m., sparking concern from those nearby who witnessed the increase in frenzied activity at MacDill. Some of these planes were part of the Composite Air Strike Force (CASF). Colonel Dave Willits, the information officer for TAC, gave unclear answers as members of the press asked him about the uptick in activity. Willits claimed that the CASF planes that had just arrived came to MacDill on a regularly scheduled rotation and not in response to escalating tensions with Cuba. In a story on the front page of the October 18 *St. Petersburg Times*, Willits told reporters that "MacDill is a new field (for TAC) and I'm sure they're down there getting to know the field." According to a front-page article in the October 18 *Evening Independent*, St. Petersburg's afternoon newspaper, an officer assured reporters in the room that these confidential exercises "are planned far in advance and it is only coincidence that this exercise took place at the same time as the U.S. Navy and Air Force buildups" elsewhere in Florida. MacDill became part of TAC's jurisdiction on July 1, 1962 after ten years of being run by Strategic Air Command (SAC). In an October 16, 2002 *St. Petersburg Times* article commemorating the fortieth anniversary of the crisis, Robert Sumner recalled his time stationed at MacDill while serving with U.S. Strike Command in the Air Force. He remembered that aircraft flew over MacDill and the Interbay Peninsula of Tampa around the clock and the region "was full of troops." Involved in high-level conversations at that time, Sumner said unequivocally that forces in MacDill and throughout Florida were prepared to engage in nuclear combat if the Soviets ever launched weapons toward the United States.

Despite public pronouncements to the contrary, those who came onto MacDill during the summer and fall of 1962 knew that the increased movement on the base amounted to more than a new round of training exercises. An October 25, 1992 article in the *Tampa Tribune* recalled the frenzied activities that *Tribune* photographer Art Thomas witnessed when he drove into MacDill on October 17. From his vehicle, he saw multiple fire trucks follow each large airplane as it landed. The fire trucks then repositioned themselves to follow the next plane that prepared to land. Along with *Tribune* reporter Ron Sustana, Thomas also witnessed enlisted men stocking hangers with multiple rows of bombs. The public information officer told them, "It's just a little exercise—perfectly normal." Activity at MacDill increased on October 19. Strategic Air Command (SAC) members went through a number of "alert" exercises and security increased around the perimeter of the base. For many hours, telephone calls made to the base did not connect. Although signs outside the entry gates at MacDill may have said "Security Condition Normal," activities on the busy campus indicated otherwise.

Fortifications covered the entire base. Steve Otto, a longtime writer for the *Tampa Tribune,* shared a story with readers on October 13, 2002, about events along the water near MacDill almost forty years earlier. At that time, Ron Kolwak, a young employee with Tampa's afternoon paper, the *Tampa Times*, wanted to learn if rumors of missiles and artillery equipment occupying the coastline at MacDill were true. Kolwak and two other newspaper employees hopped onto his seventeen-foot boat with cameras in hand. As they sailed at a moderate distance from the shore, they saw an extensive array of weapons, antiaircraft rockets, and radar systems. They also noticed soldiers looking their direction and pointing weapons at their boat. As they pulled away with the 100-horsepower engine running at full speed, they heard tracer bullets fall into the bay just behind them as the boat raced up Hillsborough Bay to Davis Islands, successfully eluding a Tampa police patrol boat. Kolwak learned that troops at MacDill meant business, as he later discovered that an officer at MacDill had ordered in no uncertain terms for military forces to blow up their boat.

The Floridan Hotel in downtown hotel swarmed with nearly 200 military personnel who arrived during the missile crisis. Another nearby hotel, the Tampa Terrace, also filled with troops who prepared for possible deployment to Cuba. Robert Saunders, the field secretary for the National Association for the Advancement of Colored People (NAACP) in Florida, spent time in Tampa investigating whether some hotels openly discriminated against black military personnel sent to Tampa since many private businesses and accommodations continued to operate segregated facilities. Indeed, at the same time soldiers of all races prepared for war, battles at lunch counters in Tallahassee and other parts of Florida signified a different struggle.

Political battles also dominated headlines. Hoping to secure his re-election in the November 6 election, U.S. Representative William C. Cramer used the escalating situation in Cuba as a way to condemn Kennedy and Democrats in Congress. Cramer, one of the few Republicans in Florida politics at the time, hoped to restore the two-party system at a time when conservative Democrats held control in the Solid South. The October 16 *Clearwater Sun* mentioned a gathering where he spoke in front of 200 Pinellas and Pasco Republicans about his opposition to plans for the expansion of the original Dependents' Medical Care Act of 1956 into a broader form of social insurance that later became Medicare. Regarding Cuba, he lambasted Kennedy for letting Americans "rot in prisons" while claiming Kennedy kowtowed to Castro.

Prior to the public having full awareness of the Cuban blockade, Cramer regularly characterized Kennedy and other Democrats as weak and ineffectual. While speaking in Madeira Beach at the Holiday Isles Women's Republican Club, Cramer said that Kennedy's tactics amounted to little more than "powderpuff action" against the Soviets. The October 18 *St. Petersburg Times* reported Cramer's strong insistence that the Kennedy Administration grant formal recognition to the Cuban government in exile. Cramer proclaimed that Kennedy had succumbed to "Khrushchev doctrine" while abandoning the Monroe Doctrine. In campaign mode, continued his criticism of Kennedy a couple of days later at a Republican fish fry near Lake Maggiore in southern St. Petersburg that attracted nearly 1200, as described in the October 20 *St. Petersburg Times*. Cramer condemned the New Frontier programs of Kennedy and American foreign policy in Cuba, Laos, and along the Berlin Wall as reasons for the world to "laugh at us." Along with claiming that Kennedy "has been off the job more than any President in this country's history" and not available during times of crisis, Cramer punched from the other side by stating that Kennedy "needs some backbone and intestinal fortitude." Despite the failure of the Bay of Pigs incursion eighteen months earlier, Cramer called for America to sponsor another invasion of Cuba by exiles. At a Republican rally in Clearwater Beach, Cramer reassured supporters that Russian missiles in Cuba could not hit the Suncoast directly, because they had a minimum range, per Cramer, of 350 miles. This came as news to officials in Washington, D.C., especially since the trajectory of a missile could become shorter depending on the angle from which it is launched.

Cramer and other critics changed their tone as tensions escalated and public officials sought to maintain calm. An August 6, 1995 article in the *Tampa Tribune* recalled some of the paranoia as tensions increased. The massive increase in troops and fears of nuclear war led some private citizens to stock and hoard food and supplies, while others talked about digging fallout shelters—something difficult to do in an area where many properties sit close to sea level—and schools resumed duck-and-cover exercises. Tampa mayor Julian Lane urged calm and restraint as he quickly returned from a mayors' meeting in Miami during the crisis. An October 25, 1992 article by Leland Hawes of the *Tampa Tribune* recounted that Lane pledged "Tampans will be as safe in their native city as any place they can go. To panic would be foolish." As Lane sought to downplay fears, the Tampa police department's pledge to monitor "aliens" elevated suspicions in a city with a large Cuban American population. When news leaked out that managers of Tampa's Lowry Park Zoo had considered plans to put down the zoo's animal population to prevent them from wildly roaming through nearby neighborhoods in the aftermath of an attack, fears transformed into absurdities.

Despite the militarization that took place at MacDill, residents of the Tampa Bay region did their best to maintain composure even as tensions remained high. News reports mentioned that many residents throughout the Tampa Bay region had purchased large numbers of canned goods, first aid supplies, candles, and similar items. Gun and ammunition sales also spiked. Gas stations raised the cost of a gallon of gas by about five or six cents a gallon, to 35-38 cents, an unusually high price. Students and parents affiliated with Sacred Heart Academy, a Catholic school in Tampa, gathered in the school's auditorium on Sundays during the fall of 1962 to pray and practice evacuation maneuvers, according to a May 13, 2012 *Tampa Tribune* story. Another *Tribune* reporter wrote in the September 27, 2009 issue about students at Robinson High School who recalled how the constant hum from aircraft landing at MacDill drowned out the words of their teachers throughout the missile crisis. A November 9, 1996 article in the *Tribune* mentioned the Mumbauer family of Keysville, in rural east-central Hillsborough County, that decided to construct a fifteen-by-thirty-foot bomb shelter during the crisis out of cinderblocks with a roof made of lumber from an old phosphate mine. This shelter has two sleeping areas with surplus bunk beds, a bathroom, and a bicycle connected to a fan that could circulate the air. Stocked with canned water and food during the missile crisis, less than a decade later this shelter became a swimming pool after the family removed the roof.

Preparations continued as the crisis entered its second week. Civil Defense units throughout the region distributed pamphlets and expanded patrols. According to an article on the front page of the October 24 *Evening Independent*, St. Petersburg City Manager Lynn Andrews claimed the city's Civil Defense plans were adequate and promised to implement "a public information program on how to build, improvise, or supply fallout shelters." Meanwhile, Assistant Superintendent Paul D. Bauder of the Pinellas School Board of Public Instruction said that parents of the district's 62,000 students could not rely on the county to provide buses to get their children home in the event of hostilities. He added, "Parents should make a plan of the route their children are to use in walking home. They should also plan ... on protection ... watching out for fallen wires and ducking for cover." The front page of the October 25 *Evening Independent* showed students at St. Petersburg's Euclid Elementary School crouched in duck-and-cover exercises, while mentioning that the youngsters also practiced evacuation exercises to the "safest parts of the building" in case of sirens. Such drills became commonplace throughout areas schools.

Fears escalated. Administrators at Shorecrest School, a private St. Petersburg institution, sent pupils home on October 24. Incidents of stockpiling of food, supplies, and ammunition increased, with a manager of St. Petersburg's Montgomery Ward department store noting the "terrific" sales of survivalist gear and ammunition sales at ten times their regular pace. Similar trends happened at other stores, including Webb's City, a large complex of stores under single ownership in downtown St. Petersburg. Attendance at church masses at St. Jude the Apostle Cathedral in western St. Petersburg reportedly doubled, and large crowds attended an around-the-clock prayer vigil at another church. WSUN-Channel 38, the city's television station headquartered at the Million-Dollar Pier, pre-empted early evening programming to air a Civil Defense film, "Florida's Operation Survival." WEDU-Channel 3, the region's educational television station, also planned to run a series of Civil Defense programs in late October. Meanwhile, concern also grew along the Gulf coast about the prospect of Russian trawlers competing with Florida fishing fleets in open international waters. Since foreign vessels in these waters did not fall under catch limits imposed upon American ships, fear grew that Russian boats anchored at Cuba might overfish and harm Florida's harvests from the seas.

At this time, Florida Presbyterian College (FPC) sat along Bayboro Harbor on its temporary home. On October 18, trustees planned to vote on whether they would admit academically qualified students of all races. They did approve this measure. As FPC students planned to move to their new, permanent campus near Maximo, an increased military presence surrounded the former Maritime Base. On October 28, soldiers from Camp Johnson in Louisiana came to the base. Their landing craft docked in Bayboro Harbor, alongside the campus. Soldiers in this detachment could not take liberty within the city and had to remain encamped on the Navy Reserve's USS Greenwood, a destroyer escort, and USS Beaufort, a patrol boat. Although some of the soldiers visited the college campus, the October 29 issue of the *St. Petersburg Times* clearly stated that students and other civilians had to keep their distance from the soldiers. One student told a reporter that "if we talk to them we're expelled from school and if they talk to us they're court-martialed." Meanwhile, on the same day these troops arrived at Bayboro, students at Florida Presbyterian held a sendoff for one of their own, a 19-year-old with the first name of Tomás, who received a "draft" request from Cuban Revolutionary Forces in Miami to go to that city and train in a U.S.-sponsored unit of Spanish-speaking Cubans interested in fighting to remove Castro. As Tomás left the campus to catch a bus to Miami, many FPC students cheered him on with signs saying "Castro, no! Tomás, sí!" and "Give Fidel Hell, Tomás!"

Media coverage relied on reports from the wire services about events elsewhere, while mixing local interest stories with carefully written and redacted accounts of activities at MacDill. The October 23 issue of the *St. Petersburg Times* had the large headline "President Quarantines Cuba; U.S. Forces Guard Caribbean." Throughout the day on October 22, TAC reconnaissance planes arrived at MacDill. At times, they arrived in intervals of five to ten minutes. The TAC planes replaced a fleet of older B-47 Stratojets redeployed to Hunter Air Force Base at Savannah, Georgia. Also on October 22, large caravans of transport vehicles stuffed with munitions arrived at MacDill accompanied by police escorts as they drove along Dale Mabry Highway. Although the official statements asserted that the munitions were planned for exercises at the Avon Park bombing range in Florida, many believed that they were brought in case needed in a combat situation with Cuba.

Tension filled the air at MacDill on October 28. According to articles in the August 6, 1995 and October 21, 2012 issues of the *Tampa Tribune,* crews picked up a signal from a radar system on the morning of Sunday, October 28, falsely indicating that a missile launched from Cuba was on its way toward Tampa. Commanders at Strategic Air Command, already concerned about a surprise attack and on DEFCON 2 heightened alert since October 24 in anticipation of a possible nuclear war, worried that this unidentified object might strike Tampa or another site near MacDill. Fortunately, as American planes flew overhead with nuclear rockets armed and ready, the enlisted personnel and civilian officers averted conflagration. They stood down rather than responding to what amounted to be a false reading on the radar satellite system, one caused by a test scenario on a magnetic computer tape rather than actual missiles.

The large headline on the Friday, October 26 edition of the *Clearwater Sun* proclaimed, "Banner Winter Season Seen," with a prominent photograph of the beach dominating nearly forty percent of the front page. In much smaller font on the right column, a subtitle announced, "Cuban Crisis Viewed Having Little Effect" on this issue, the twenty-fifth annual 'mailaway' edition for locals to send to their snowbird friends 'back home.' According the Joseph Cornelius, the Bank of Clearwater's president, "This should be an excellent season on Clearwater Beach despite international tensions. The sun, the sand, and the water still beckon our northern friends." Ed Norvell, manager of the Jack Tar [Fort] Harrison Hotel, the largest in the city, agreed, "The West Coast of Florida will not be affected in any way at this time by the Cuban crisis." An editorial in the same day's edition reflected similar optimism, claiming that Florida and the Suncoast had "fewer targets of significance in war potential" regardless of their close proximity to Cuba. Adding that the area showed no signs of imminent distress, the editorial continued, "Folks are staying put, visitors are arriving daily, there is no panic buying and it's been business as usual."

In reality, those old enough to remember living in the Tampa Bay region during the Cuban Missile Crisis suffered many tense moments and sleepless nights. Planes soared overhead, convoys clogged major arteries, alarms blasted at all hours, and duck-and-cover drills became daily exercises. As the immediacy of the threat disappeared, residents resumed their preparations for the fall Holiday and tourist season, merchants hoped for another banner year, and snowbirds began to arrive. *La Gaceta*, Tampa's tri-lingual newspaper that had captured the pulse of the Latino and Italian immigrant communities for decades, continued to follow news of Castro's consolidation of power and dealings with the Russians, but without an excited or jingoistic tone found in other publications. By the early months of 1963, mention of the missile buildup in Cuba faded away in most Tampa Bay publications as Cuban Americans along the Suncoast departed from the few remaining cigar industries into new lines of work and moved from older enclaves to newer neighborhoods. As Ybor City suffered decline during the 1960s and 1970s, Tampa's unique ethnic mix of Cuban, Spanish, and Italian tastes transformed Columbus Drive into a new and vibrant "Boliche Boulevard."

The most profound and enduring legacy of the Cuban Missile Crisis in the Tampa Bay region involved the strengthened ties between the military and local enterprises. MacDill, once a candidate for closure in 1960, expanded its role as military installation with extensive geopolitical significance. Similarly, defense-related industries working in partnership and under contract with federal departments enjoyed newfound opportunities for expansion. Although the Suncoast has changed dramatically since those nail-biting days in October 1962, the legacy of that time remains an important part of the region's history, even as regularly scheduled nonstop airline service has now resumed between Tampa's airport and Cuba and the long-embargoed St. Petersburg-Habana Yacht Race that ran from 1930 through 1959 began again in 2017.

ABBREVIATED BIBLIOGRAPHY

Clearwater Sun, October 1962.

[Tampa] *La Gaceta,* January 1963-March 1963.

Jarvis, Eric. "A Plague in Paradise: Public Health and Public Relations during the 1962 Encephalitis Epidemic in St. Petersburg." *Florida Historical Quarterly* 85 (Spring 2007): 371-397.

Pizzo, Tony. "Tampa's Cuban Heritage." *Tampa Bay History* 16 (Spring/Summer 1994): 40-47.

[St. Petersburg] *Evening Independent,* October 1962.

St. Petersburg Times, 1962, 2000-2012.

Tampa Tribune, 1992-2016.

"Tony Pizzo's Ybor City: An Interview with Tony Pizzo." *Tampa Bay History* 16 (Spring/Summer 1994): 22-39.

Yglesias, José. "The Radical Latino Island of the South." *Tampa Bay History* 18 (Spring/Summer 1996): 71-74.

CHAPTER 5

Southeast Florida
during the Cuban Missile Crisis of 1962

BY JOE KNETSCH

"They were loaded down with what looked like missiles and missile apparatus together with such equipment that was to operate a military site, i.e. generators, and trucks. Living on the perimeter of this now low key military base and on the railroad feeding it was like having a front row center seat to a war."

Blair Connor

Imagine tromping through the Everglades hunting the ever-elusive pythons and finally seeing a hawk, but it is not the kind of hawk you would expect to find in this remote wilderness and National Park. It is a Hawk missile emplacement left over from the Cuban Missile Crisis of 1962. Later you find out that this was not the only missile site in the Everglades and that the entire region was surrounded by such bases. Nike bases also were established, some of them lasting into the 1970s. More research discloses that radar installations were also cropping up, some large and obvious and others more or less hidden in the vegetation covered areas, or islands, in these same Everglades. In the distance, you can almost hear the ammunition exploding and what sounds like gun-fire going off. You may have imagined the secret training bases of the Cuban exiles getting ready to infiltrate Cuba for another try to oust Fidel Castro from power. You may even dream of the V20 boats headed south to land these same infiltrators in some hidden cove along the Cuban coast. All of these scenarios were reflections of the reality of South Florida during the harrowing days of the Cuban Missile Crisis.

A young Blair Connor recalls the trauma when the seemingly endless trains passed by his home in Opa Locka, "It was a busy week or two at the little railroad station across the street from our house. Numerous long trains came and went (two or three a day). They were not the standard ten or eleven freight cars but were of enormous length, maybe a half mile or more in length." In addition to slowing down local traffic the presented a clear picture of the preparations for war. Connor continued, "They were loaded down with what looked like missiles and missile apparatus together with such equipment that was to operate a military site, i.e. generators, and trucks. Living on the perimeter of this now low key military base and on the railroad feeding it was like having a front row center seat to a war." What Blair Connor and most others did not know, Opa Locka was one of the more important centers of activity in those days, the local headquarters of all CIA activity and the debriefing center for Cuban refugees and exiles.

Another worry for Opa Locka residents were the giant "Flying Boxcars" or air transport planes that rumbled over their houses and shook everything inside not nailed down. So low did these planes fly, especially during take-off, that many residents could make out the pilots in the cockpits as they flew just above tree-top level with their heavy cargoes. Many of planes were loaded with medical supplies to assist the corpsmen who would, it was believed, soon be needed with an invasion of Cuba. Connor's good friend, Frank de Mello, was in the

Air Force Reserve unit from Opa Locka and was activated on the first day of the crisis. De Mello drove a medical supply truck, and during these hectic days, he traveled twice a day to and from Homestead Air Force base delivering the supplies for the expected invasion. Most of the convoys in which De Mello took part were large, at least fifty trucks in number, and some were eighteen wheelers. It was a constant flow of supplies to the main center for operations in Southeast Florida, Homestead Air Force Base. Casual traffic was discouraged in the vicinity of military bases and the main routes to and from each.

As in all such cases, the reactions of people differed depending upon age, occupation at the time, location, and family involvement. Most of those who were children at the time remembered the dive under the desk routine and some of their memories are rather amusing. Marta Darby, interviewed on NPR on October 22, 2012 by Michel Martin, remembered, "Like it wasn't enough that we thought the world was already ending, they would have—we started to do these drills. And I know it was just that week because it never really happened again. They would kind of turn on the fire alarms, say OK, when you hear the alarm, you dive under your desk. And I remember, even as a child, thinking, like, really? This is going to prevent a bomb from destroying us?" She also remembered the family discussions about the events of that first week and her parents wondering where would the missiles strike first? As she noted, "it was a sort of surreal conversation. I was very afraid." Nineteen-year-old Nate Conner from Becket, Massachusetts, was assigned to the Second Missile Battalion, Fifty-Second Air Defense Artillery, stationed in Carol City in northern Dade County. "We knew the missiles were live. Somewhere in the back of my mind was the thought that something could happen. In the motor pool, they told us to get under a large truck. But I wasn't scared." If he wasn't scared, he was one of the few lucky ones. Henry Mack, then a former commander of one of the Nike-Hercules bases, remembered being ready psychologically for the task of defense but, he recalled, "I did not think about killing people. But I hoped I would not be the first to fire. I absolutely knew it would be a holocaust." Everyone had differing memories of that time, however, each prepared in their own way, scared or not.

The Army responded to the Missile Crisis with alacrity but most of the units that arrived in Southeastern Florida came after the main crisis was over. Many of the units that came direct to Florida came from Fort Bliss, Texas, via railroad. These were part of Army Sixth Group, including Nate Conner's group which included a headquarters battery, four Nike-Hercules field batteries and a security unit. This group was associated with the Strategic Army Corps (STRAC) and was trained to respond to national emergencies within seventy-two hours. The distinctive unit insignia "*Semper Paratus*" means "Always Prepared" and it apparently was, however, transportation problems delayed the arrival until about October 31. Other units from throughout the United States came via the Florida East Coast Railway and some experienced delays because of the amount of military traffic suddenly thrust upon the line. Truck and equipment convoys experienced similar delays also. Part of the reason for the delays and general lack of immediate protection was the assumption by the military that Florida, having little in the way of strategic industry, would not be a major target. Cuba, although a pain in the side of American policy, was not considered a launch area for Soviet aggression. However, with the rise of Castro and his turn to the Soviets for aid and defense, the threat should have been anticipated, but wasn't. Hence, Florida was relatively defenseless against the arrival of missiles in Cuba.

Citizens seeing the arrival of the troops via train and highways began to stock up on any available materials needed to survive an attack, nuclear or otherwise. Many grocery stores and small country outlets were swamped by the local population eager to obtain provisions, batteries, flashlights, charcoal, and other necessities they might need in an emergency, similar to the normal preparations made for an approaching hurricane. This meant local traffic arteries were clogged and local provisions were not available to the troops coming into the region.

This situation meant that provisions not available locally had to be shipped in via the same routes that were already clogged with troops, equipment and missiles arriving to defend this area. Although, given the nature of the emergency, some of this disjointedness could be expected, the lack of coordination with local authorities in the beginning contributed to the confusion and delay. One of the more interesting cases was the stopping of the trucks loaded down with equipment by the state police with warning tickets issued for overweight limits, poor lights and other code violations. The truck drivers were then issued telephone numbers to call in case this happened. However, once the first missiles were assembled and batteries fully operational, the police then became the official escorts of these same trucks and helped them whisk their valuable cargoes towards Homestead and other destinations. All sites and batteries were fully operational by November 14. Although the alleged date of the end of the crisis is often given as October 28, the reality is much later, when the Soviet bombers were removed and shipped back to the Soviet Union, beginning in late November. As many of the missiles set up in Florida were designed to knock down Soviet bombers and other conventional aircraft, and American military leaders stressed the necessity of continuing the buildup of military might in Southeastern Florida.

Most of the early missile sites in Florida were equipped with conventional weapons and not the more dangerous nuclear missiles, which came later. Part of the reason for the delay of delivery of the nuclear tipped weapons was the requirement that each site had to be inspected first and pass the test for internal security and proper external security. Rolls of concertina wire placed upon conventional fencing did not qualify as sound security, and nuclear-equipped sites required more than this. Missile batteries had to have certification prior to installation of the more powerful weapons. Each site was required to have an inner security area within an area commonly known as the exclusion area, which was guarded not only by armed men but specially trained military policemen and dogs. The quick construction of missile sites in

Southeastern Florida did not allow time for them to be made secure enough to pass the certification tests. Most of the sites saw their staff arrive via rail late at night with minimal equipment to guard or set up the complete site. To say the least, many of the sites were originally quite primitive.

Normally, sites were set up to guard strategic cities and industries, however, since Florida generally lacked these, the first batteries were built on the edge of the Everglades and in other less populated areas. Some were lucky enough to set up near settlements, like Princeton, and actually had minimal structures to house command units. The Princeton location offered the old B & L Farms' tomato packing house. Most other units were not as fortunate. In most cases, the men were housed in tents without flooring, in areas that often flooded during the frequent afternoon rain showers. Some locations were so poorly placed it was necessary to haul in sand and gravel to build up the land so the men would not be sleeping in water. Potable water was difficult to come by and much of it had to be trucked into the camp sites from outside sources. Most meals were cooked over open camp fires or gas ranges and consisted of the usual GI fare eaten from their mess kits. Shaving required some of the men to invert their helmets and use cold water trucked in from nearby fire hydrants to insure clean water. The local water, which came from the Everglades or flowed south from heavily populated areas, was not safe enough to use for cooking or shaving. Bathing was almost out of the question in some areas until showers were installed and supplied by water from the outside. Some brave souls swam in the canals to get somewhat clean, however, as most Floridians know, these canals are hardly safe places in which to swim given the high bacteria counts, alligators, and the presence of poisonous snakes. Luckily, they did not have to worry about pythons or boa constrictors, which thrived in the area by the late 1990s.

President Kennedy was worried about the Florida airfields being too open to the general public and too removed from a war footing to provide sufficient precautions against an aerial attack. He wanted the planes, men, and equipment more dispersed, as normally done when a nation is on alert. Kennedy, remembering perhaps the problems at Pearl Harbor and Manila at the beginning of WW II, was concerned that the planes would be lined up wing-tip to wing-tip making them easy targets. Admiral Robert S. Dennison was asked his opinion about the situation, and he replied that he preferred to let things be in the name of efficiency. Kennedy did not buy that argument and asked for some aerial photography of our fields. The situation was as he feared and mirrored the Soviet alignment in Cuba—wing-tip to wing-tip and highly vulnerable to attack. The president then asked that some of the smaller airports, like West Palm Beach, be used to help disperse the planes and assigned Roswell Gilpatrick to resolve the situation. By the end of October, some of the smaller installations were being made ready for use by the newly arrived twenty-four air wings assigned to Florida for a possible confrontation with the Soviets in Cuba. Kennedy would later recognize the importance of the air wings by making presentations to various units at Homestead and in the Keys.

The men stationed in Southeastern Florida suffered from the heat, the lack of potable water and the insufferable insects. Daily rats, snakes and spiders invaded the tents of the men making many of the more squeamish than before. Rats, in particular, were a problem, often overrunning some of the sites to such an extent so that men took turns at night to fight off the rodents. In other camps, the problem was so bad the men took to shooting the rats with small arms. Most camps also had to keep portable generators running to maintain the equipment and provide electricity to run the few lights that were strung up for safety. The army did try and make life more tolerable for these men as quickly as possible, but budgets and the logistics of the problem sometimes delayed putting in the wooden floors, shower stalls and wooden walkways to travel between the tents and the equipment. Morale suffered because of the poor conditions, and the fact that most of the men were on temporary duty with no knowledge of when they would return to their more permanent stations made the morale problem worse.

The state was not lacking for action during the crisis as the later U-2 flights originated from bases in the state. Almost all reconnaissance flights over Cuba and those watching the Soviet ships approaching the demarcation line where they would encounter the U. S. Atlantic fleet on quarantine duty were managed from Key West as part of the Joint Air Reconnaissance Coordination Center (JARCC). As the crisis grew and the military went into DEFCON III status, thirteen percent of the Strategic Air Command (SAC) was in the skies above on a continuous basis. The Joint Chiefs of Staff were getting the final operational plans ready for implementation at this time and were working out the details of a possible "surgical air strike" on the missile sites in Cuba, possibly to be followed by an invasion. President Kennedy was originally favorable to the idea but soon became much more cautious, especially after General Walter C. Sweeney advised him that there could be no guarantee that such a strike could eliminate the missiles without killing Soviet forces and causing damage to nearby Cuban populations, thus causing a possible "hot war' to explode. Hence, the president sided with the quarantine idea much to the dismay of some of the JCS. As far as Florida was concerned, it would now be a prime target for Soviet missiles since the state was the base of operations for a possible invasion of its Cuban ally. Photo missions were also continued from Florida on a timely basis with the Navy's East Coast Composite Carrier Photo Squadron flying out of the Key West Naval Air Station and flying the results to the Jacksonville Aerial Photo Laboratory for processing. The first low-level flights disclosed in detail the construction of the missile sites in Cuba and so crucial were the photos that the air commander, George Eckard was ferried to Washington D. C. to personally debrief the president on the findings. For a state that had been all but ignored in the planning of the nation's air defense system, Florida now became the virtual center of most activity and much of it centered on Southeastern Florida.

Florida also became the center for the effort to broadcast propaganda into Cuba to remind them of the freedoms they had lost. The main "experimental" air station, run by the Army's Signal Corps, was stationed in Flamingo on the southern tip of the Florida mainland. This station worked in conjunction with the CIA's efforts at broadcasting news, propaganda and disinformation into Cuba. One of the largest operations took place at the Dry Tortugas National Park when a ship bearing a large transmitter stationed itself there and began broadcasting. This activity supplemented the continual Voice of America broadcasts but with more political information than VOC offered. This new station later moved to Sugarloaf Key after the main crisis was over. Other CIA sponsored stations appeared from time to time in the Keys during the crisis. Exile Cubans also operated "pirate radio" stations throughout the Keys and along the southern coast of the state. Indeed, many of these were there to transmit orders/directions to cover forces landed in Cuba from time to time, with or without CIA training or sanction. The Keys also became the base for some of the other covert operations of the exile community, many sponsored or encouraged by the CIA. Training of exile commandos was done at Cape Sable during the crisis and after and other training exercises conducted at various points in the National Park. Southeastern Florida was the hub of such activity in the state, a point not lost on Castro's intelligence community.

The changes brought by such a focus on Southeastern Florida were many. Some of the missile sites established at this time became part of parks, school site locations, and other public venues. Part of the old Battery B Nike site became the administrative headquarters for Dagney Johnson Key Largo Hammock State Park. Part of the Crocodile Lake National Wildlife Refuge was once a launch site for a section of Battery B. You can now visit a portion of old Battery A's position while visiting Everglades National park. Most famously the site of old Battery D became known as the Krome Avenue Detention Center where people deemed mentally incapable, criminal or those to be deported were detained and is now part of the Homeland Security Detention Facility.

Some of the radar installations are still active. The improvements in the infrastructure demanded by the Department of Defense have been made, including some of the vast interstate road system so often accredited to President Eisenhower. Some of the fire towers, like that on Long Pine Key are remnants of this time period too. Radio Marti and Marti TV have used facilities on Cudjoe Key for many years to broadcast uncensored news into Cuba. Many improvements took place at Homestead AFB during and after the crisis, and this base became the center for cleanup operations after Hurricane Andrew. Indeed, it was on the verge of being closed in the early 1960s until the crisis stirred interest in the base and highlighted the need to keep it open. Many improvements in Key West owed their origins to the Cuban Missile Crisis, including increased security measures at the Truman Annex. In Miami, many of the boat yards benefited greatly from the increased orders from the CIA and other security agencies and operations. Improvements at Port Everglades and the Port of Miami were also undertaken at these two ports in Florida. The list could go on, but the reader will sense that the Cuban Missile Crisis played a significant role in the development of Southeastern Florida as the premier area for growth in the state and, for a while in the 1960s, the nation.

ABBREVIATED BIBLIOGRAPHY

Public Papers of the Presidents of the United States: John F. Kennedy ... January 1 to December 31, 1962. Washington D. C. United States Government Printing Office, 1963.

Carter, Charles D. "Cold War Missiles (Nuclear) in Miami, 1962-1979." *Nike Historical Society.* http://nikemissile.org/ColdWar/CharlesCarter/CubanCrisis.shtml.

Blair Connor. "Cuban Missile Crisis of 1962." *North Miami Historical Society Newsletter.* 2011. (By permission of the author)

Hach, Steve. "Cold War in South Florida: Historical Resource Study." *National Park Service, Southeast Regional Office, Atlanta, Georgia.* October 2004. [http://www.nps.gov.]

Patterson, Thomas G. "Fixation with Cuba: The Bay of Pigs, Missile Crisis and Covert War Against Castro." http://jfk.hood.edu/collec-tions/Weisburgh%20subject%20index%Files/.../item20%050.pdf.

Martin, Michel (Host). "Childhood Memories of the Cuban Missile Crisis." NPR Broadcast, October 22, 2012. http://www.npr.org/2012/10/22/163395079/childhoode-memories

CHAPTER 6

The Cuban Missile Crisis
Along the Northeast Coast

By Robert Redd

"…when the teacher called roll you had to say here and show your dog tag around your neck. When we were in school we thought they were cool, not realizing that they were to identify our little bodies if we got bombed, lordy!"

Ray Hargis

The year 1962 started out much like any other year in the area around Daytona Beach. February brought the good ol' boys to Daytona Beach for the annual running of the Daytona 500. Over 50,000 were in attendance to watch the race on February 18 as Edward "Fireball" Roberts lived up to his nickname and took home the trophy in what was then known as the NASCAR Grand National Series. His performance was a dominating one, leading 144 out of 200 laps and defeating runner-up Richard Petty by twenty-seven seconds, a margin unheard of in today's superspeedway racing. The year proved to be a good one for Roberts as he won two races and garnered the pole seven times. His second victory of the year was also on the high banks of Daytona International Speedway during the Firecracker 250 held on July 4.

Fireball Roberts earned his nickname while in high school pitching for the Zellwood Mud Hens in an American Legion league. His fastball was almost unhittable. A professional baseball career was never in the cards however and after being discharged from the U.S. Army Air Corps due to asthma, Roberts began his racing career in earnest. Roberts raced in 206 Grand National Series races, amassing 33 wins and 32 poles. Perhaps more impressive was that he finished in the top-ten more than 59 percent of the time he raced. Roberts' career was cut short when he passed away as a result of injuries sustained in a fiery crash at the Charlotte Motor Speedway in 1964. His legacy has been long remembered however and in 1998 he was named one of NASCAR's 50 greatest drivers and in 2014 the highest honor in NASCAR was bestowed upon him as he was elected to their Hall of Fame.

As spring turned to summer the joys of baseball season flooded through the coastal areas. From little leagues all the way through the highest levels of minor league ball, fans flocked to stadiums to cheer their favorite teams.

Daytona Beach served as home to the Islanders, an A ball level minor league team affiliated with the Kansas City Athletics playing their first season in the city. Led by future major leaguers such as Burt Campanaris and Tony LaRussa, the team amassed a 61-61 record. To the north in Jacksonville the Cleveland Indians AAA level minor league team, the Suns, compiled an excellent 94-60 record behind the efforts of future major league pitchers Tommy John and Louis Tiant. The Suns won the International League pennant in 1962 and defeated the Rochester Red Wings, a Baltimore Orioles farm team, in the first round of the playoffs by winning four games in a best of seven series. They next fell to the St. Louis Cardinals farm team, the

Atlanta Crackers, by the same four to three margin however and just missed out on the Governor's Cup.

Other regular tourist related events such as Bike Week in March and spring break festivities during March and April went off without a hitch. NBC News anchor Chet Huntley, in a report titled *Daytona Beach: Where the Boys Went,* discovered the still new phenomenon known as Spring Break. What he found was in many ways similar to what might be seen today. Huntley described students and their "determined and almost fierce pursuit of fun as though it were about to be outlawed or go out of style." This fun included dancing, particularly the Twist, the Holly Golly, and the Mashed Potato. There seemed to be very little touching, and beer drinking, as much as thirty cans a day, was a popular activity. The report did however show that alcohol was prevalent on the beach whereas today alcohol is not permitted on Daytona Beach.

All was not fun and games on the beach however. Students expressed worries; some more important concerns than others. Conformity, and fitting into adult society and finding a job after graduation, was on the minds of some. Many of the students however understood the world they were going to inherit. Theirs was the first generation to truly deal with the threat of global nuclear war. One student expressed his concern, "I'm scared. I'm scared to death."

What Chet Huntley ultimately determined though is what most adults will discover about youth of this age range. He figured the students were, "Neither as wicked as we fear nor as good as we might wish."

Employment in the area was led by the Florida East Coast Railway in New Smyrna Beach and the new General Electric plant which opened in Daytona Beach in 1962. Tourism dominated the St. Augustine area as it still does today while Jacksonville was on the cusp of a population explosion in part due to the creation of the Jacksonville Port Authority and the jobs that came with the expansion.

As October arrived the summer heat was starting to break in Florida. Another type of heat was about to kick in however. Late Saturday, October 13, 1962 Major Richard Heyser flew his U-2 spy plane at a height of over 70,000 feet over Cuba bringing back the first photographic evidence of Soviet missiles on Cuban soil when he landed in Florida on Sunday. Howard Palmer of Mandarin, a neighborhood in Jacksonville, remembered for an article in the October 21, 2012 *Florida Times-Union*, "I was 21 during the Cuban Missile Crisis, in the Navy and stationed at NAS Jacksonville in a photo reconnaissance squadron. I believe it was the weekend of around October 14, 1962. The Squadron Duty Officer came tearing into the office demanding to know if I could work on the Crusader camera gear! I told him I could. …I saw the Russian missiles on the ground in Cuba! …I later found out that our XO [Executive Officer] delivered those prints, showing the Russian missiles in Cuba, directly to President Kennedy!" This evidence helped eventually lead the world's superpowers to the brink of nuclear war; a war that could have ended life on planet earth as we know it.

Despite the evidence provided by Major Heyser's flight, President Kennedy wanted further proof of the Soviet and Cuban military build-up and the extent of it. He received it when on October 23 six RF-8 Crusader jets from the Light Photographic Squadron Number 62 departed the naval air station at Key West. These low flying planes flew close to the sea in order to avoid detection. Led by squadron leader William Ecker the pilots flew in groups of two recording images from approximately one thousand feet in elevation. The pilots were able to record much clearer images of missiles, missile erectors, fuel trucks, building construction, and even images of the workers themselves, than Heyser had brought back. When the pilots returned to Jacksonville Naval Air Station and the film was developed, the images left no doubt as to what the United States was dealing with. As soon as the negatives were developed they were flown to Washington D.C., with Commander Ecker in tow, for meetings with the Joint Chiefs of Staff.

President John F. Kennedy would find himself in a difficult situation. It was important to keep the communists from emerging victorious in Latin America. While the Joseph McCarthy "red scare" was a thing of the past, to be seen as soft on communism would be a death knell to Kennedy's political career. Less than two years prior he had given the go-ahead to a dramatic failure known as the Bay of Pigs. This attempt to oust Fidel Castro failed for many reasons including a blown cover for the operation, a lack of supply line for the troops on the ground, and a lack of support from the Cuban people themselves. Kennedy could not fail again.

On October 22 Kennedy addressed the nation, bringing all citizens information about the various types of weaponry it was believed the Soviets were placing on soil just ninety miles from the United States. The next few days were perhaps the most-tense in American history as Kennedy issued orders for a naval quarantine with a demand that all missiles and bombers be removed. The ball was now in the court of Nikita Khrushchev and the Soviet Union.

United States military forces increased throughout the state. Crews from the Jacksonville Naval Air Station were on high alert. Flights from there provided a constant stream of surveillance around the island of Cuba while fighter planes were prepared for possible use. The Naval Station Mayport, another major installation in the Jacksonville area, served as a home for the Second Marine Division. In addition to men, Mayport had a large amount of military hardware at the ready including five aircraft carriers, five LSTs, ten destroyers, two destroyer tenders, two attack cargo ships, two oilers, one dock landing ship, thirty-two Marine helicopters and their crews, along with other supplies. Contrary to rumors, Navy dependents living in the Jacksonville area were never evacuated.

As tensions mounted civilians were able to see for themselves the military build-up that was occurring. For cities such as Jacksonville with a major military presence one could see the increases in soldiers, military equipment and supplies, and the tightening of security. For those in other cities all it took was watching the roads, skies, and railroad tracks.

Jamie Montgomery recounted a story for the *Florida Times-Union* about train loads of soldiers being sent south, "he and hundreds of other soldiers rod [*sic*] in a passenger train from Fort Lewis, Washington. The train kept clothes over the windows so citizens would not see soldiers in the train cars. He said that other trains, from other locations across the U.S. met at the Jacksonville Train Terminal where, during the night, all the soldiers were loaded on a train and sent to South Florida." Many locals can vividly remember seeing these trainloads of young soldiers being transported south."

For many who lived through the crisis the troop movements are a memory that is still fresh. There were varied ways for troops and materials to go south whether by rail, by road, or by water. It is interesting to view the varied memories people have of this action. Alice Clay Benedict of Samsula recalled, "All the missiles that were sent to south Florida passed through New Smyrna Beach on US1/Dixie Freeway. You could see all the tanks, missiles, conveys and troops headed to south Florida as they passed through our town."

Janet Mooney remembered how her family was reminded of other critical times in our nation's past, "Troop trains headed South on the FEC [Florida East Coast Railway] tracks, my mother saying it reminded her of WWII." Irvan Owens recalled being in school and witnessing the convoys headed south, "I was in school at NSB's [New Smyrna Beach] old [L]ive [O]ak high school at that time and we would look at the FEC railroad and all you could see was dust flying from the trains going real fast south all day with soldiers setting on flat cars with rifle racks and equipment headed to the Orange Bowl for staging area, this was a hair-raising time to say the least!" Murray Brown recalled the array of items being shipped by rail, "I well remember the trains, one after another, going south, loaded with troops, big guns and all kinds of vehicles. You could watch them all day from the old high school (the real old high school on Live Oak)." Mike Usina can remember the trains rolling through the St. Augustine area, "Back then we lived just off Ponce Blvd. Had a clear view of the FEC railroad tracks, for days on end train load after train load of military equipment was going south. I also was working for Fairchild aircraft and we were working a lot of overtime getting the planes finished that were in the hangers."

The railroad was certainly a vital mode of military transport and Jean Swebilius remembered the extra precautions that were made to protect it in the New Smyrna Beach area, "I remember armed soldiers standing and I assume protecting the railroad crossing at Canal St." Skip Caldwell can also remember precautions that were taken near the railway:

> I was 15 at the time, My Dad was at the main fire station working. I was a volunteer and at times I helped on fires and/ or around the Fire House. Notification came in that the Troop Trains would be coming through nonstop for over 24 hrs. The city did not have a fire station, at that time, on the west side of the tracks. My Dad and I and someone else took a pumper over to the West side of the tracks on Highway 44, which was along West Canal St. back then. We sat in and slept up in the back on the hoses; for over 24 hrs. I was right there up near the tracks watching missiles, Cannons, tanks, and a whole bunch of people go clickity-clack, clickity-clack nonstop.

While memories of river transport are not as prevalent, some locals such as Carol Spangler recalled the almost clandestine efforts along the Intracoastal Waterway, "I remember the boats with the men going south for the Cuba crisis, it was pitch black on the river sat on the dock and waved to the guys going by...it was scary." Marty Seng recalled, "I remember PT boats running down the river" and Joy Hemingway remembered, "the Navy going down the river. I sat on the dock and waved for hours!!"

For some, such as Tom Read, the troop movements created an inconvenience to the normal routine, "I remember not being able to get across US1 for hours and hours." Richard Bowers recalled these delays also, "One train after another, in many cases, between trains there was not enough time for cars to cross the tracks." Others such as Susan Galbreath remembered the excitement teen girls had in seeing the brave men in uniform, "Now I have a picture in my mind of watching (from the field behind the high school) the convoys going south. I remember waving and flirting with the soldiers!"

What became apparent to Floridians was the need to prepare. How to successfully prepare for a nuclear war was something that did not seem to be realistically on the minds of most at the time. Floridians learned that they were not prepared should war come to the United States. The local newspapers such as the *Pelican*, out of New Smyrna Beach, ran several articles with suggestions from the Civil Defense office suggesting a stock of supplies such as powdered milk, fruit and vegetable juices, canned fruits and vegetables, dry cereals, soft drinks, coffee and tea, bottled water, first aid kits, amusements for the children, paper supplies, candles, and of course, tobacco. Whether the tobacco was to smoke or use as a form of currency was not stated. It is only with 20/20 hindsight that we can realize how futile those efforts would have proven if nuclear war had come

For many, who were students at the time, one of the clearest memories of the crisis was the school drill of climbing under their school desks for protection. Stephanie Tumblin Farquhar recalled the crisis from a New Smyrna Beach elementary school perspective, "All I remember as a child in Faulkner St. Elementary is the missile drills. We had to get under our desks with our hands over our heads. There was one day when school was optional because 'something' was going to happen between USA and Cuba. I don't remember what was supposed to happen however I did get to stay home from school that day." Jeff Clark remembered things slightly different at Faulkner Street Elementary, "We had Civil Defense Drills once a week, the alarm bell was deeper in sound than the fire alarm bell. We marched to the semi-basement at Faulkner and had a blanket and some canned goods...like that would help us if they nuked the Cape." Tim Klecan also remembers a lower level at Faulkner St. Elementary, "I was in first grade at Faulkner Street Elementary. Mrs. Mathews. About all I remember is going to the lower level and hunkering down. It was in October 1962—not real sure what day. As 6-7-year-olds we were clueless as to the gravity of it all. Thank God for His mercy and protection that day. We might have just been in a drill that day. It's hard to remember but I remember going down in the basement." Ray Hargis recalled a detail not mentioned by others; dog tags that students wore, [and] "...when the teacher called roll you had to say here and show your dog tag around your neck. When we were in school we thought they were cool, not realizing that they were to identify our little bodies if we got bombed, lordy!" With the passing of more than fifty years some Faulkner St. students remembered having the tags while others do not. In an article in the *Florida Times-Union* newspaper out of Jacksonville, Deborah Burmester Leibecki remembered that at Justina Elementary School in Jacksonville, "We were also given metal bracelets that had our full name, address, religious faith, phone number and mother's name on it. I still have mine after all these years."

Other local schools had similar drills for students as recalled by students of the era. Elynn Gillespie Clevenger recalled, "I remember the drills at Read Pattillo Elementary & having to hide under our small wooden desks." A sentiment echoed a bit more graphically by Nancy Jo Baker who remembered the scene like this, "Read Patillo [sic] only had us get under our desks, and cover with a large white towel. I remember asking the teacher why a white towel. She said it would reflect any radiation. Quick answer I bought it. Then asked an older cousin.

Found out it was to show blood." Extra precautions were taken at Read Pattillo as remembered by Becky Pope, "Besides getting under our desks in the drills, we had black out curtains at Read Pattillo." Colleen Bresnahan Odonnell also remembered that the "curtains were to save us from all the flying glass from the big windows that we had instead of air conditioning!"

Students at the now closed Samsula Elementary, a bit to the west of New Smyrna Beach, had to partake in drills as well as recalled by Jodi Zeitz Carr, "Samsula Elementary School also had regular air raid drills. We were instructed to crouch under our desks and fold our arms over our heads."

To the south in Oak Hill students like Tina Farless recall the seriousness of the situation in the way that only a young student would remember it, "I was in Burns Elementary in Oak Hill. We had bomb drills—get under your desk with your hands over your face. If we heard a loud bang and saw a mushroom cloud [we were to] lay flat against the wall." Donia Adele DeWees recalled school in Oak Hill during the crisis with a bit of humor, "but we did have drills often where we did have to get under out desks. We did not have to learn any Spanish...I went to the Oak Hill School. Maybe they thought us Rednecks could defend ourselves?"

In DeLand, Colleen Affeld recalled "Remember the civil defense drills at school in DeLand's George Marks Elementary." Some teachers were more graphic than others as remembered by Donna Craig from Daytona Beach, "I was in Daytona at the time. I remember hearing about one of the junior high teachers sending her seventh-grade students home one day saying she didn't expect to see any of them the next day. Needless to say, those kids were traumatized!"

Students were expected to help make preparations should an attack ever happen. Canned goods and water were stored at local schools so should an emergency happen and the students couldn't leave there would be preparations. Colleen Affeld remembered "We had to bring in canned goods and teacher kept them in back of room in case we were stuck there." Ann Jones told a similar story about school in New Smyrna Beach, "Faulkner Street Elementary also had us bring blankets, jugs of water and such in case we had to stay at school due to civil defense issues." Anne Pickhardt recalled how things ran at Read Pattillo Elementary in New Smyrna Beach, "…and [we had to] have a change of clothes, a gallon of water, and some canned food in our cubbies." Pat Stubbs Krewson explained the confusion that some students felt in having to have supplies at school, "I remember the drills, blackout curtains and having to bring in canned food—thought it was for hurricanes—had no idea [what it was really for] 'til years later!"

An interesting and insightful aspect of the crisis was seen in articles in local newspapers with high school students as the focus. The *Daytona Beach Morning Journal* ran an article titled *How SHS [Seabreeze High School] Students View Cuban Crisis*. Reporter Peter Fiero asked several Seabreeze High School students the question "What do you think about the Cuban situation?" The answers showed a distinct support for U.S. policy. John Graham answered, "The U.S. should do everything in its power to keep our hemisphere free from communism. If necessary, we should use force to keep it free." Calista Fofee was proud to say, "It's good to know that at last the U.S. isn't going to back down. This alone has helped us greatly and won us new credibility in the world." New Smyrna Beach High School student Susan Galbreath, who was to later become a successful journalism teacher, wrote a regular column for the *New Smyrna Beach News* titled *Suzzie Says* and in it she put forth the idea, "President Kennedy has realized that you can't continue compromising with the Reds. He has realized that there has to be a stop somewhere. Perhaps Cuba is the place. Perhaps Russia will retaliate with a bomb or perhaps we have frightened her by showing our teeth. But whether we keep the so called 'peace' we live in today or not, we young people who are tomorrows [sic] leaders, must and will support President Kennedy."

Stress and fear were a constant in people's lives. Some dealt with it better than others and most parents tried to keep the seriousness of the situation from their children. Some were more successful than others. Annmarie Smith told the story of her mother, "My mother, Joyce Grissom Smith, told me about how stressful that time was. My parents had just bought a new house in Jax Beach and were preparing it to move in. She was 8 months pregnant, with a 2-year-old, and an eight-year-old. She would walk on the beach, and could see the Navy ships from Mayport out to sea. There were a lot of them, and it really brought the danger home to her." Janet Mooney of New Smyrna Beach remembered, "The nervousness of the adults was felt by NSB's children." Shelly Broadway also picked up on the nervousness of adults, "My family moved to NSB in 1958. I also attended Faulkner elementary. The only one that was scaring me was my mother." Deborah Burmester Leibecki of Atlantic Beach remembers, "I can remember my parents watching Walter Cronkite on our black-and-white TV and, whenever my brothers or myself walked in the room, they would turn it off or change the channel My brothers and I knew something was up, but our parents wouldn't talk about it." Lea Craig recalled a relative who lived with the memories of the crisis his entire life, "My cousin in St. Augustine was frightened beyond repair and (this is no joke) was never quite the same after that scare. He talked about the Cuban Missile Crisis until he passed away—not a lot, but it would come up now and then."

Residents of the coastal areas certainly feared for their safety and with good reason. The mystery of what was actually in Cuba and who had access to launch a nuclear assault was more than enough to cause concern for oneself and loved ones whether young or old. Local news outlets at times attempted to squash these fears. The *Daytona Beach Morning Journal* on October 27, 1962 ran an article titled *Missiles in Cuba Can't*

Hit Here. The article quoted local Representatives [Albert] Herlong and [William] Cramer who had met with both State Department and Defense Department officials in Washington D.C. In a telegram they said, "We discussed the missile threat to Central and South Florida and it was determined to be minimal. It is accepted generally that while the medium range missiles are able to go as far 1,020 nautical miles, they also have a minimum range of 350 nautical miles. ... Therefore, the only threat to Central and South Florida would be by Russian planes and the U.S. military buildup and detection system is ample."

Despite the attempted reassurances of politicians who no doubt had good hearts, the people were concerned and wanting to protect themselves. Bomb shelters became a fashionable home add-on despite the fact they were probably of limited value in the event of nuclear attack. Doug McGinnis recalled a local concrete company having a prototype shelter on display, "Rinkers (or whatever it was called then) had a model bomb shelter on display." Sales were probably brisk. In Flagler County the *Morning News Journal* reported there were two county owned shelters with room for over 1,300 persons. In a bit of unreasonable optimism, the Flagler County Commission reported, "with the aid of some free labor and some donated material [we] are building shelters for all of the population." While the shelters would have provided only limited protection in the event of a nuclear war, the shelters made people feel safe, as recounted somewhat bluntly by Barbara Hunt Apodaca, "It was comforting to know we had a place to go if Florida blew up." In more recent times the now abandoned shelters are still to be found. Charlie Hillyer and friends figured out what to do with an abandoned shelter, "I am a Jacksonville native, living in St. Johns County. An elaborate bomb shelter was built at a friend's house. We found its value some years later as a gathering place for teenage parties."

While life continued normally in many ways, some security changes could be seen; particularly the precautions taken at local airports. Stephany Tumblin Farquhar remembers, "My husband lived on the airport property—behind what is now Lost Lagoon. He said private and commercial planes in large numbers were parked all over the airport property as they were not allowed to fly any farther south than here." In Daytona Beach, the *Morning Journal* reported that "As a security precaution, FAA facilities at City Airport has [sic] been restricted to 'authorized personnel.'" It was reported that the order came from Washington D.C. and applied to all control towers and FAA facilities.

As news of the Soviet Union withdrawing from Cuba was announced, fears began subsiding and life returned to normal. While there were still fears of nuclear war and the "duck and cover" drills still occurred in schools, life began to be less scary. The train loads of soldiers heading south were no longer seen. The Civil Defense calls for stockpiling supplies were halted.

For some cities, the post-crisis years were a boom. Daytona Beach, for instance, had the new General Electric manufacturing facility that according to GE leader Paul G. Fritachel could easily change from space industry development to weaponry should hostilities arise again and the founding of the Jacksonville Port Authority in 1963 which replaced the city's Department of Docks and Terminals helped lead to a population and economic boom in the city as the shipping industry expanded. Other cities, such as New Smyrna Beach, suffered. The Florida East Coast Railway workers went on strike in early 1963. New Smyrna Beach was a major rail hub between Jacksonville and Miami and many FEC employees called New Smyrna Beach home. The strike, which helped ultimately end FEC passenger service, caused many men to uproot their families in order to find work elsewhere, such as the Brevard County area with the burgeoning space program.

Normal events happened in 1963, NASCAR ran the Daytona 500 with substitute driver Tiny Lund winning and etching his name on the Harley J. Earl Trophy; spring training came to and major league teams left Florida; minor league baseball teams played across the state with players dreaming of hitting the big time; and spring break crowds continued to grow at various Florida locations. Good times were returning, but trouble was just a few months ahead. Viet Nam would become the surrogate for the anticipated clash between communism and capitalism.

ABBREVIATED BIBLIOGRAPHY

http://www.nbcnews.com/video/rock-center/46662820#46662820

Daytona Beach *Morning Journal*

Florida Times-Union

Facebook: Minorcan Facebook Group

Facebook: You Know You're From New Smyrna Beach When...

CHAPTER 7

Civil Defense and Governor Farris Bryant

BY JOE KNETSCH

"For Florida, at least, the last few days have molded a memory which should forever dispel the reaction to civil defense which starts, 'but it can't happen here', ... It can. It could. It may yet. We must be ready."

Farris Bryant

"That autumn day in 1962, my mother pulled our station wagon, brimming with provisions, into the carport," remembered Karen Bjorneby, "Our neighbor was outside, in red lipstick, and black stretch-pants, smoking a cigarette and watching her two sons ... she came to help with the groceries, when my mother asked if her husband, too, had gotten a call, she laughed. She wasn't worried, she said, it was all just posturing. And, if not, she shrugged, we'd all be dead anyway." The neighbor was planning for only one thing, Halloween, not self-preservation or the protection of her sons and husband. Meanwhile, Karen's mother continued to stock up and move the canned soup, spam, cookies and peanut butter into the basement just in case the neighbor was wrong.

Sleeping bags, Coleman lanterns and water were the order of the day deep in the basement. That night, October 22, 1962, President John F. Kennedy announced to the world that the Soviet Union had moved ballistic missiles within striking distance of the United States on the island nation of Cuba. It would shake the confidence of many and create a crisis atmosphere felt throughout the world.

Civil Defense, something nearly forgotten in these hectic days, quickly came to the fore. What to do about Castro and the Russians soon took a back seat to the questions as to how best defend our families, especially in vulnerable states like Florida, just ninety miles off the Cuban coast. Florida's governor, Farris Bryant, was deeply concerned about this problem and pushed many initiatives toward the legislature. Bryant was deeply involved with the training of Cuban exiles and was given a steady flow of information regarding the affairs in Cuba, indeed, he may have known about the missiles about the same time as Senator Kenneth Keating, a Republican Senator from New York, whose nationally published statements were a constant thorn in the Kennedy administration's side. Keating, it appears, was getting raw data from the exile community and publishing it nationally and Bryant seems to have had the same or similar access to this information. One source even went so far as to state that during the Governor's Conference Bryant was going to expose the existence of the missiles in Cuba but was dissuaded by members of the Kennedy team. Whichever may have been the case, Governor Bryant was deeply concerned with the dangers to his state. In late 1961, Bryant, just returned from a tourism promotional tour in Europe where he encountered Danes who were worried about missiles coming across the Fehmarn Strait from East Germany thereby ending Denmark's notable peace initiatives. Bryant noted this encounter, "Yet their concern was not greater than that of those citizens of Florida who have written and who continue to write me expressing their alarm over the rumors and stories they have heard that missiles stand poised in nearby Cuba, ready to streak across the Straits of Florida to devastate this peninsula and its people."

He immediately set about getting the state ready by encouraging preparedness and preparation for any eventuality coming from Cuba.

Governor Bryant was aware that the Eisenhower administration had let civil defense matters slip into the background and had relied upon a defense policy of "massive retaliation" to prevent any attacks on the United States. From the creation of the Federal Civil Defense Administration under Truman, the commitment to civil defense had been more window-dressing than actuality. Few in Congress agreed that any such agency was needed and cut the appropriation requests asked for by both the Truman and Eisenhower administrations to the point of insignificance. Under both these administrations, as the situation in Korea began to stabilize, the interests and commitment to civil defense waned. Ironically, considering the later national role to be played by Governor Bryant, former Florida governor Millard Caldwell, headed the FCDA for the first few years. Caldwell, who had limited experience in Washington circles, continually put forth the ultimate dollar amount needed, as recommended by his staff, and that number was astronomical for the era. To quote B. Wayne Blanchard's study of American Civil Defense Policies, "For years, civil defense would suffer because of the Director's statement that it would take $300 billion to provide a comprehensive civil defense system in the United States." Caldwell also approached Congress with a combative attitude that did not endear him to the committee chairmen, something that carried over to his staff when appearing in front of the Congressional committees. The lack of staff analysis, a proposal on how many lives might be saved by the program being proposed and other issues made it impossible for Congress to rationally consider the $300 billion proposal which was presented as "merely adequate' for the purposes noted. Congress, and later the Eisenhower administration, then took the attitude that civil defense should be a state and local responsibility, not a federal program. Proposals to start a nationwide shelter system soon fell by the way side and civil defense, when appropriations were allotted at all, was put on the back burner.

The Eisenhower administration pursued a policy of massive evacuation, especially after the Soviet Union had exploded its first hydrogen bomb in 1953. The newly appointed Civil Defense Director, Val Peterson, reasoned that evacuation would be the best solution since the main cities would soon be obliterated by the explosion of such massive devices. Within months of the announcement of the new policy, the BRAVO hydrogen explosion revealed the extent to which massive radioactive fall-out would drift in the atmosphere and cover thousands of miles of territory, making a mockery of massive evacuations. Fall-out shelter planning was limited to trying to find the best materials and where to construct them so as to avoid the most danger from the fall-out. Throughout the next couple of years, the Eisenhower administration stuck with this program, if such it really was, until Senator Estes Kefauver's Armed Services Committee in the Senate and Representative Chet Holifield's Military Operations Subcommittee in the House started to raise serious questions concerning the lack of planned civil defense. Holifield was particularly concerned with the creation of a national shelter program to support as many citizens as possible in case of nuclear attack. Peterson's appearances in front of these committees and others did not go well but not nearly as poor as Caldwell's. Within Congress itself, there were severe differences of opinion and the Appropriations Committee in each house constantly cut whatever funding was requested. Congress took the civil defense debates to a higher level pushing the Eisenhower administration to propose a new level of joint work with federal and state officials working together to come up with a plan. The result was the 1957 appointment of Security Resources Panel of the Science Advisory Committee which became known as the "Gaither Committee." Besides recommending more research and development of various defensive missile systems (Intercontinental Ballistic Missiles, etc.) and an increase in conventional forces, they also put forth the idea of a national fallout shelter program to protect the civil population. The price tag for this system would be approximately $25 billion over a number of years. Unfortunately, Eisenhower personally did not agree with this recommendation since it contradicted his policy of seeking a balanced budget and economy in government. The recommendations of the stellar committee went nowhere. Many in Congress agreed with this lack of support, including many in the military who referred to the shelter program as a "manifestation of a 'Maginot line' mentality."

The newly elected president, John F. Kennedy, had pushed hard for a better policy toward Cuba, accusing the Eisenhower administration of being soft on the question and of allowing Castro to remain in power. He, by implication, made a point of noting the lack of preparedness for nuclear attack and expressed agreement with the Gaither Committee recommendations regarding some facets of the civil defense program. Immediately after taking the reins of power, Kennedy was faced with the Bay of Pigs, which proved to be a disaster of tremendous proportions and the Berlin Crisis, which soon resulted in the building of the infamous wall. His appointment of Frank Ellis to head up his civil defense initiative was a near disaster too in that Ellis quickly proposed a "revival for survival" and a visit to the Pope to secure the use of churches for fallout shelters. A vague reference to civil defense and individual responsibility for fallout shelters led to more criticism and the creation of a fallout shelter "scare" in mid-1961. Kennedy quickly moved to correct this error and moved the civil defense apparatus into the Pentagon under the new office of Civil Defense headed by the very capable Stewart Pittman. It made the new office highly visible and more important than in the past. To emphasize his point, Kennedy noted that civil defense could not prevent a surprise attack, guarantee against obsolescence or destruction, or be obtained on the cheap. He did note that a nation prepared to protect its citizens would give any opponent second thoughts about launching such attacks for fear of retaliation by the survivors. He also said something that is always true in international politics, "But this deterrent concept assumes rational calculations by rational men. And the history of this planet is sufficient to remind us of the possibilities of an irrational attack, a miscalculation, or an accidental war which cannot be either foreseen or deterred. It is on this basis that civil defense can be justified – an insurance for the civilian population in the event of such a miscalculation." And the president continued, "It is insurance which we can never forgive ourselves for foregoing in the event of catastrophe." Kennedy then asked, through Pittman, for a supplement to the budget for $207.6 million for civil defense—and got it! For the first time in the post-war era, the Congress approved the entire request for the new Office of Civil Defense which immediately instituted a national survey for fallout shelter needs and space. The Cuban Missile Crisis would put an exclamation point on the need for civil defense. For his role in helping to shape the legislation for civil defense, President Kennedy sent Governor Bryant a personal telegram thanking him for his efforts.

The rapid increase in Cuban migration to Florida in the early 1960s focused Governor Bryant, an ardent anti-communist, on the problem of Cuba and its relation to the growth of the Sunshine State. As governor, one of his first steps was to overhaul the overlooked potential of civil defense in Florida and make it a priority of his administration, along with highways and education. Civil defense had not been a priority of previous administrations but then, none of these had faced the immigration problems brought on Florida by the Cuban exodus. Bryant went to Key West and observed some of the craft upon which these freedom seekers traveled in to escape Castro's regime. He could not believe that twenty to twenty-two people could fit into a fourteen to sixteen-foot vessel and sail to safety to Florida from Cuba. He immediately set up a program to provide full assistance to the refugees who settled, mostly, in the Miami area. He also issued an executive order that required his immediate staff, and himself, to take a formal twelve-hour personal survival course. This became the model for thousands of Floridians who learned via educational television, one of the first such courses televised statewide. In this effort, Florida led the nation in making civil defense something reachable by the majority of its population. His initiative in using educational television to spread the civil defense message was important, and he was able to assure President Kennedy, when called to the White House for a briefing on the crisis in October of 1962, that Florida stood ready to react to any emergency. Upon returning to Florida after this meeting, he broadcast to the state the results of this conference and what it meant to the people of the state. By keeping citizens informed, he also helped the civil defense effort by preventing any wide-spread panic. In this effort, Governor Bryant had the able assistance of Chairman Stan Witwer of St. Petersburg, chair of the Educational Television Commission, and Kenneth Small, executive Secretary of the Florida Association of Broadcasters. As he said in his televised address to Floridians, "For Florida, at least, the last few days have molded a memory which should forever dispel the reaction to civil defense which starts, 'but it can't happen here', ... It can. It could. It may yet. We must be ready."

With the arrival of over 100,000 troops, twenty-four complete air wings and numerous support staff and civilian contractors, Florida's economy had an instant boost. It also brought, again, the eyes of the nation on the Sunshine State and its potential. The governor took to the national air waves to assure the nation that Florida was still a safe place to visit and encouraged many to come see for themselves the beauties and possibilities of living in Florida. He also protested against the removal of the meeting of the Interstate Oil Compact Commission from Florida during the crisis noting that there was no immediate danger to the delegates of this thirty-member organization for the conservation of oil and gas reserves. The crisis was short-term and did not really impact the ability of Florida to host conventions, meetings or enjoy the beaches. As normality returned, so should the tourists to Florida's wonderful climate. The campaign had an immediate impact and the 1962-63 tourist season set a new record.

The governor also took the opportunity to strengthen the Florida National Guard with new equipment, reorganization, and additional disaster preparedness training. The disaster preparedness included the maintenance military order, support for civil control, order during a crisis, and how to best utilize the Guard's resources during a natural disaster, a role that the Guard proudly continues to play in our state. Although the Guard was not called up during the Missile Crisis, in the usual sense, it was put on full alert and provided support assistance to the heavily concentrated troops brought into the state during the emergency. Bryant also saw the funding for three new armories approved and the creation of the Military Museum and Archives in the home of the Florida Guard, the St. Francis Barracks complex in St. Augustine. Bryant was especially proud of his accomplishments in improving the training and equipment for the Guard, a major and necessary component of civil defense.

It was a prescient move by Governor Bryant to increase the state's role in civil defense because once the crisis had passed with the missiles being removed, Congress reverted to its old ways and cut civil defense appropriations. The chairman of the committee on appropriations was Congressman Albert Thomas who did not believe that the civil defense programs proposed by the Kennedy administration would work or were worthwhile. He did not believe that large cities, like Washington D. C. could be evacuated in less than two weeks and he did not believe that sheltering people in the big cities would work at any time. From his interviews with the mayor of Hamburg, Germany, who survived the bombings of World War II, he learned that the best place to be during such raids would be outside, away from falling buildings. Also, stockpiling of drugs, food and other survival supplies was a wasted effort. All of these things could be had already, at any time, at the corner drugstore, of which, he noted, were "everywhere." The final budget submitted by the Kennedy administration, lacking a strong push by the president, was slashed by Thomas's committee and never reached the full House or Senate intact. State and local governments (and private individuals) would have to take up the slack.

The debate on civil defense was nationwide and sometimes acrimonious. At the Governors' Conference in Hersey, Pennsylvania in mid-1962, Stewart Pittman and others produced the results of the national civil defense survey first proposed by President Kennedy in 1961. Bryant, who was vice-chairman of the National Governors' Conference Committee on Civil Defense (Nelson Rockefeller of New York, was the chairman), was in the audience to hear that sixty-eight percent of Americans surveyed by Elmo Roper and Associates favored including shelter space in new and larger buildings and seventy-seven percent favored the proposed Federal Shelter Incentive Program to assist schools, hospitals and colleges to meet the costs of expanding their shelter facilities. A whopping eighty-six percent agreed that government should bring more of its spaces in existing buildings into the program and that shelters should be stocked with emergency supplies for a possible two-weeks stay. The Federal survey found that there were shelter spaces for about sixty million people available at the time of the survey. In the most revealing "show and tell" of the day, the Department of Defense brought out charts indicating that of those likely to survive the immediate heat and blast of a nuclear attack, forty to one-hundred-and-twenty million people would, without shelter protection, die from fallout. Some in the audience took comfort that regardless of the size of the attack, the nation, as a whole, would not be destroyed. The majority of the governors present felt that the need for immediate action could be seen in such a scenario and agreed to push for more funding for fallout protection for their constituents.

Back home, Bryant worked with his staff, including his director of Civil Defense, H. W. Tarkington, on a plan to improve the state's ability to protect its citizens. One of the first actions was the creation of a communications center in the basement of the new building recently completed for the Trustees of the Internal Improvement Trust Fund. The director of the Trustees' staff would act as the office manager within the new headquarters. However, the size of the basement precluded any large-scale evacuation center and was limited to the Trustees (i.e. the governor and cabinet and their immediate principal assistants) and staff. The basement would resemble a miniature war room, almost identical to those found in the White House or at White Hall, with maps, communications equipment and food/supplies for at least two weeks. At least three transmitters and three receivers would occupy some of the pace, one each for the Highway Patrol, the amateur radio state-wide net and the amateur radio network in the immediate twelve county area. One portable cot would be utilized by two people assigned to the center. Of course, there would be a radioactive monitor ready for use at any time. The windows would be covered by at least five hundred sand bags provided by the State Road Department. The reasoning behind the exclusive headquarters was to prevent the Governor and Cabinet from being swept up in the confusion and chaos of the first hours and days after the expected attack. From the leadership perspective, this was a rational and reasonable plan although not everyone would agree.

Although not considered a part of Civil Defense, Bryant was National Chairman of the National Council on Cold War Education, an arm of the Governors' Conference. Bryant took this seriously and soon instituted a new course to teach Florida's students about the dangers of communism and the values of Americanism. The course was to be called Americanism vs. Communism and was made mandatory for all students in Florida's schools. The course had to be completed successfully by each student before graduation from high school. It was instituted in 1961 for the first time on a statewide basis. For the governor, this course was to teach the basics of citizenship and the responsibilities of being a citizen in a democracy. Some concern as to the reception of this course was expressed by Secretary of Education, Thomas Bailey so the governor decided to call a Conference on Cold War Education on July 18, 1962. Working through the Institute for American Strategy, a non-profit educational organization seeking to foster an idea of the communist threat to American values and democracy, Bryant called in a number of recognized national experts on the dangers of communism to instruct teachers, administrators and private organizations. The attendees were expected to pay for their own transportation and hotels (it was held in Miami Beach) and a twenty-dollar registration fee. Because it was not a free conference it was not expected to draw any more than two to three hundred at the most. When more than one thousand people showed up at the Americana Hotel, the organizers were dumbfounded and surprised. It was a huge success and showed the governor and the state that there was a great concern for the problem of having a communist country only ninety miles from our shores. Bryant assigned some of his staff, especially John Evans who later became the Director of the Florida Center for Cold War Education, to find other such initiatives in the nation. To their surprise there were no other such programs in existence. In 1963, a national report was issued noting the stepping stones needed to combat the growth of communism in the United States and elsewhere. It defined the goals of the National Governors' Conference on Cold War education as, "the development of knowledge essential to the understanding of America's heritage of freedom, and of the nature of the attacks upon that freedom, open and covert, by the followers of International Communism." The emphasis, according to the report for 1963, was to have the individual inform himself/herself about what it is they are fighting for and to understand that the communist countries are waging a real ideological war against the free nations of the world and that the individual must decide how he/she could best go about defeating this threat. An informed public would be the best civil defense against communism.

Special film presentations were brought into Florida to educate the students and teachers about the dangers of international communism. Nationally known scholars, like Dean Ewing Shahan of Vanderbilt University, Dr. Gerhart Niemeyer of Notre Dame and Dr. Stefan Possony of Stanford were consulted and used in these films and on campus teaching. One of the other advisors to the committee was Zbigniew Brzezinski, later National Security Advisor to President Jimmy Carter. Most of the curriculum for the course work came from the Institute for American Strategy and was funded by the Lilly

Endowment Fund of Indianapolis, Sears, Roebuck and Company and the Florida Center for Cold War Education. The curriculum consisted of using the books, *Masters of Deceit* allegedly by J. Edgar Hoover (actually done by FBI staffers) and *The Communist Manifesto* by Karl Marx and Frederick Engels. Other materials included, as of 1969, a series of film strips from the Van Swearingen Institute out of Chicago. If osmosis is a valid learning method, these film strips surely worked their magic. This author, who taught this very class from 1969-1972 can vouch for the need to have a designated "waker-upper" if viewing these films for more than fifteen minutes. It should be noted that none of the above-named scholars had any input into these films, and the course as created under these guidelines was probably not what Governor Bryant had in mind when he began the program in 1961.

One can easily grasp why Governor Bryant instituted the course that generation of students still discuss across the coffee tables. However, it was part of the overall response to the Cuban Missile Crisis of 1962 and the growing threat communism posed to America at that time. Yet, there was a downside to the crisis that few have broached, the impact it had on that generation of students and how they would perceive atomic war and the constant threat of nuclear war. Some recent commentators on this era see the beginnings of the "peace revolution" at this time and the controversial anti-war movement of the late 1960s and early 1970s. The jury is still out on this aspect of the Cuban Missile Crisis, if indeed it is one. We are sure the debate will go on for some time to come but know too that the next generation who will rewrite this history may find something totally different in this episode.

ABBREVIATED BIBLIOGRAPHY

Blanchard, Wayne. "American Civil Defense 1945-1984: The Evolution of Programs and Policies." *National Emergency Center*. Emmitsburg, Maryland. Monograph Series, Volume 2, No. 2, 1985.

Evans, John. "Time for Florida: Report on the Administration of Farris Bryant, Governor of Florida, 1961-1965." Tallahassee, Florida. Center for Cold War Education, 1965.

Mast, Robert H. *Impact of the Cuban Missile Crisis: Patterns of Public Response*. Washington D. C. Office of Civil Defense, Office of the Secretary of the Army, February 1966.

The Farris Bryant Papers. Florida State Archives, Tallahassee, Florida.

CHAPTER 8

A Communist Cuba
with Missiles on West Florida Minds

BY DEAN DEBOLT

*"In World War II, Hitler sank 150 ships in the Caribbean Sea and
the Gulf of Mexico with 40 submarines [and that] Khrushchev has
400 submarines, each of which is infinitely better than Hitler's and
which carry missiles with atomic warheads."*

Congressman Bob Sikes

In August 1962, Senator Kenneth Keating informed the U. S. Senate
that there was evidence of Soviet missile installations in Cuba, which
was later confirmed by photographs from U-2 flyovers of the island in
mid-October.

But in the days before what would be known as the Cuban Missile
Crisis, Floridians had other things on their minds. The Pensacola newspapers noted the increasing hostilities in a region known as Vietnam,
the concern over developing Hurricane Ella, and the string of launch
failures at Cape Canaveral. An explosion of a Minuteman ICBM on

launch at the Cape was noted as "the most awesome rocket failure ever seen here."

Of even more concern for Pensacola were the circulating rumors of the demise of naval aviation and possible cutbacks in training at the Pensacola Naval Air Station. These were denied by the Secretary of the Navy Fred Korth in a visit to Pensacola on October 13-14. This brought great relief to Pensacola. The *Pensacola Journal* editorial of October 16, 1962 stated that "he painted a bright picture of naval aviation."

In Fort Walton Beach, Eglin Air Force Base was busy conducting experiments in the upper atmosphere. These chemical release experiments were under the auspices of the Air Force Cambridge Research Laboratories and were accomplished by launching of rockets by the Air Proving Ground Center's Deputy for Aerospace Systems Testing.

But the increasing national attention on Cuba did not escape the notice of Panhandle readers. The lead editorial of the *Pensacola Journal* on Saturday, October 20, 1962 was titled "What To Do About Cuba?" Readers were told of the issues involving Cuba: the missile sites, the Cuban refugees arriving in South Florida, the question about invading the island, and the diplomatic wrangling over anti-Castro policies. The suggested solution was simple—topple the Castro administration. It was not a local editorial, having been reprinted from the *Minneapolis Tribune,* but no doubt reflected the tenor of the conservative base of West Florida.

Congressman Robert L. F. Sikes, who represented West Florida as Florida's First Congressional District, spoke at the annual conference of the Florida State Beekeepers Association in Bristol on October 20. He urged the formation of a Cuban government-in-exile with recognition by the United States. Arming and training of Cuban ground forces would be necessary, and certainly American troops along with planes and ships would back them in their invasion to retake their homeland.

It was perhaps a strange topic in an address to beekeepers, but a strong indication that Cuba occupied the minds of many in Florida.

MONDAY, OCTOBER 22, 1962

News agencies and reporters began to take notice of unusual Washington activity late on Sunday, October 21, and these reports were shared across the nation in Monday morning newspapers. The *Pensacola Journal* shared the Associated Press story about "Sensational Moves in Cuba Crisis Hinted." This noted the sudden return of President Kennedy to Washington from California, the unusual early-in-their-offices, or staying close to their desks of Pentagon officials, the Secretary of State, and others.

Reporting agencies noted some ships moving out of Norfolk as well as some movements of aircraft and troops to South Florida. Panhandle papers reported that military authorities had assured them that the ships were going out to sea to ride out Hurricane Ella or heading to participate in the previously-planned Caribbean maneuver activities involving 40 ships and 20,000 men.

In Key West, the Associated Press reported that a group of Marines had come into the Key West Naval Air Station during the weekend and that all leaves had been cancelled. In addition, readiness drills at Mayport Naval Station in Jacksonville and at the Strategic Air Command base in Tampa over the weekend also fueled rumors about military moves. These were explained as planned and normal military activities by the Pentagon.

Most communities operated normally. Fort Walton Beach was eagerly awaiting the arrival of the King Brothers Circus as well as the opening of the movie *West Side Story* (winner of 10 Academy Awards!) at the Tringas Theatre.

Nevertheless, these reports of military moves and activity in Washington appearing on the front pages of many American Monday morning newspapers heightened worries about Cuba, especially in military communities like Pensacola.

By midday of Monday, October 22, the White House announced that President Kennedy would make a nationwide address at 5:00 Central Standard Time. The only Panhandle newspaper that published an afternoon edition, the *Pensacola News*, was able to announce this, but could only report that the President had asked for thirty minutes of television and radio time to discuss "a subject of the highest national urgency." Speculation on the topic covered all the current national and international problems including Cuba, Berlin, Southeast Asia, and the Chinese-India border war. At five o'clock, Panhandle citizens learned that the United States would blockade Cuba, preventing incoming shipments of missiles or other weapons from any country. Listeners also heard Kennedy raise the nightmare of atomic bombs being launched at the United States by Cuba, promising swift retaliation upon the Soviet Union and Cuba if this happened.

TUESDAY, OCTOBER 23, 1962

The morning Panhandle newspapers, the *Pensacola Journal* and the Fort Walton Beach *Playground Daily News*, announced the news in large, stark headlines: U. S. BLOCKADES CUBA. Little was reported of any activity at the Pensacola Naval Air Station. Instead the papers reported about the troop, air, and ship buildups in Key West, Tampa, and around South Florida.

In response to rumors that some Eglin Air Force Base personnel had been alerted as to the Cuban blockade, Eglin officials had no comment. But local monitoring of air police radio messages, gave indications that some personnel were being placed on standby alert. The 4135th Strategic Air Command (SAC) Wing at Eglin was noted as always being on alert.

The Fort Walton Beach City Council held an emergency Tuesday evening meeting. Mayor Sam Lindsey urged citizens not to panic and that in the event of a national disaster, citizens should stay home. He also asked that if children were in school, that parents leave them in the schools until officials could instruct them what actions to take. Citizens were urged to have at least a two-week supply of non-perishable food, preferably which could be consumed uncooked. School principals were also asked to stockpile food and supplies at their schools. City Manager Winston Walker advised that the city well was gas-operated and some water should be available in an emergency if not contaminated.

WEDNESDAY, OCTOBER 24, 1962

As news filtered in of military buildups in South Florida, the mobilization of Cuban forces, angry words from Moscow, support from the Organization of American States, and pledges of support from Allied countries, most West Floridians waited to see what would happen. The press reported that as many as twenty-five Soviet ships were inbound to Cuba, and many waited to see if they would honor the blockade when it went into effect at 8:00 a.m. Central Standard Time. In addition, the Pensacola and Fort Walton Beach newspapers reported the announcement by Secretary of Defense Robert McNamara that all Navy and Marine personnel would be held on active duty as much as one year beyond their normal tours. This would affect some 50,000 servicemen.

A contingent of British newsmen who had arrived at Eglin Air Force Base to do stories on the newly-arrived British Colony there (training personnel and families) were sent to South Florida by their home office.

Since Kennedy's speech had raised the specter of a nuclear war, civil defense directors in Okaloosa County reported a deluge of calls following Kennedy's address, asking for fallout shelter booklets. Additional meetings of civil defense planners were also held in Valparaiso and Fort Walton Beach.

Newspapers may have contributed to the growing uneasiness of citizens by their words and headline choices. The *Pensacola News*, in its early edition on Wednesday afternoon ran headlines such as "Blockade Underway," "25 Vessels Enroute," and "Invasion Pondered." Its later afternoon changed these to "U.S., Soviet Near Showdown In Crisis."

But most West Florida citizens were going about their normal daily lives. Okaloosa citizens cheered the news that President Kennedy had signed the bill that removed 875 acres of Santa Rosa Island from federal control, enabling them to be sold once fair market value was determined.

THURSDAY, OCTOBER 25, 1962

Thursday morning began to show some relief in the Cuban crisis when newspapers reported that some of the ships had turned back and that Nikita Khrushchev had called for a summit meeting to discuss the situation. However, Floridians were also told that the federal Office of Emergency Preparedness had dusted off its old and thick emergency Mobilization Plans from the 1950s and was proceeding to begin updating as well as planning implementation depending on the crisis.

U. S. Representative Bob Sikes had spoken to the Milton Kiwanians on Wednesday, predicting that Khrushchev would back down, and that he supported Kennedy's blockade. He expressed concern over the Cuban missile bases, but especially the idea of a Soviet submarine base near Florida. Sikes said that "in World War II, Hitler sank 150 ships in the Caribbean Sea and the Gulf of Mexico with 40 submarines [and that] Khrushchev has 400 submarines, each of which is infinitely better than Hitler's and which carry missiles with atomic warheads." He reiterated these comments again at a dinner in his honor on Thursday, October 25th in Panama City, Florida.

The *Pensacola Journal* reported that while anxiety had spread in

Pensacola on Wednesday, there was a certain calmness. There was an increase in outgoing telephone calls which Southern Bell Telephone claimed always accompanied any national crisis. People stocked up on canned goods, civil defense booklets, transistor radios, and a builder of fallout shelters had a tremendous increase in demand. A movie theater manager said it had been the worst three days they'd ever had, no business at all since Kennedy's speech. The school superintendent asked each school to activate a civil defense organization composed of teachers and students. Anxiety was eased late Wednesday when Soviet Premier Khrushchev indicated he would avoid an open clash with American ships.

Nevertheless, the *Pensacola News* reported that students had circulated the rumor that the Escambia County public schools planned to ship them by truck to Alabama in the event of an emergency. Many students telephoned their parents to come and get them, and school officials on Thursday vehemently denied these rumors. Escambia County Superintendent Dr. W. J. Woodham explained the policy was always to shelter the students at their schools in the event of an emergency. And it was reported that Eglin Air Force Base had increased its alert level but assured citizens that their activities remained in normal operation.

In Milton, the newspaper reported that their residents were in a "wait-see" pattern on the Cuban crisis.

FRIDAY, OCTOBER 26, 1962.

The Friday *Pensacola Journal* reported that the blockade would continue, but that Kennedy was open to negotiations. For perhaps the first time in a week, the paper did not use large black face type in headlines, indicating some lessening of tensions. But clearly tensions remained. The Escambia County Civil Defense Director issued a list of the 26 buildings designated as fallout shelters in the County. And a special front page note addressed to crewmen of the *U.S.S. Antietam* asked that they contact their duty office immediately for new orders. The *U.S.S. Antietam* aircraft carrier was stationed at Pensacola Naval Air Station and in use as a training ship for naval aviation.

The afternoon *Pensacola News* noted that a Soviet-chartered Lebanese freighter had been boarded and searched. But for Pensacola as well as Milton, Florida, the Cuban crisis took a back seat to the annual Navy Day, set for Saturday, October 27, with open houses at Pensacola Naval Air Station as well as Whiting Field N.A.S. A special supplement to the Pensacola paper (included in the evening *Pensacola News* of October 27 and the morning *Pensacola Journal* of October 28) contained welcoming addresses by commanders, histories of the bases, lists of exhibits, an air show by the Blue Angels, and open houses for the *U. S. S. Antietam* and *U. S. S. Tweedy* at Pensacola.

That both bases were open to the civilian population demonstrated that, at least for West Florida, these bases were not crucial at this point in time in the Cuban crisis. The only change to the Navy Day schedule appeared in the Saturday morning edition of the *Pensacola Journal* which reported that the Chief of Naval Operations Admiral George W. Anderson, Jr., had ordered a halt to tours of the *Antietam* and *Tweedy* "to prevent any possible impairment of ship' readiness for sea."

On the national and international level, negotiations continued through Sunday, October 28 and Monday, October 29, 1962, and were resolved when Premier Khrushchev agreed to dismantle the missile bases in Cuba. Florida Senator George Smathers visited Pensacola on October 29, and while he supported Kennedy and the Cuban blockade, he said our next step after the removal of the missiles should be to get rid of Castro and then communism. He said he was one of the handful of U. S. Senators briefed on the blockade by President Kennedy, and that clouds from Hurricane Ella had prevented earlier discovery from the air of the missile sites.

The blockade and air surveillance was lifted on Tuesday, October 30, 1962. Some hailed this as a victory, but others decried that the United States had failed to remove Castro. One lingering response did emerge from the crisis for Florida. On October 30, 1962, Florida Governor Farris Bryant announced a vast step-up in Florida's Civil Defense Plan, that Florida's bulky old plan had been streamlined, and he planned to call a conference of mayors, county commissioners, and civil defense directors to review the plans. He noted that 500 fallout shelters had been identified in the state, but were not marked and unknown to the populace.

The western Panhandle of Florida, during the Cuban missile crisis, were as concerned about the possibility of open warfare as many others in the state and Florida. But the distance from Cuba, and proximity of other military installations in South Florida, placed the West Florida installations in a support and backup mode rather than as frontline participants.

ABBREVIATED BIBILOGRAPHY

Pensacola Journal, October 14-30, 1962

Pensacola News, October 14-30, 1962

Playground Daily News, Fort Walton Beach, Florida, October 20-30, 1962

Panama City News-Herald, October 14-30, 1962

Santa Rosa Press-Gazette, October 14-30, 1962

Conclusion

BY NICK WYNNE

"My fellow Americans, let us take that first step. Let us...step back from the shadow of war and seek out the way of peace. And if that journey is a thousand miles, or even more, let history record that we, in this land, at this time, took the first step."

President John F. Kennedy

For two weeks in the latter part of October 1962, the world waited anxiously to see what the final outcome of the confrontation between the Soviet Union and the United States over the placement of intercontinental missiles in Cuba would be. Diplomats from all nations and international organizations manned crisis centers and exchanged apprehensive messages as they waited for the latest developments. Military leaders around the globe, aware of the potential for an accidental or deliberate nuclear exchange between these two world powers, hastily prepared contingency plans for their nations. With each passing hour, the crisis appeared to move inexorably toward "the edge of Armageddon," and the fate of the world rested precariously in the hands of two men—Kennedy and Khrushchev.

World leaders possessed an up-to-the-minute knowledge of the situation through diplomatic cables, intelligence reports, and exchanges of personal conversations, but for the average American, as well as the general world population, the paucity of news outlets and the secrecy imposed by government and military leaders meant that any knowledge they gained came from the brief evening television news programs or from local newspapers. Unlike the twenty-four-hour news cycles of today, information about what was happening was limited and, by design, somewhat placid.

For Floridians, who were on the frontline of the confrontation, tranquility in the face of the possible extermination of much of the world's population was a little more difficult to maintain. Endless convoys of troops and equipment, often tying up public transportation routes, signaled a crisis that approached that of World War II. Overhead, the flights of jet fighters and bombers reinforced the perception that war was imminent, while the hasty erection of defensive and offensive missile batteries along public thoroughfares and in remote sections of the Florida countryside was a clear indication that the Sunshine State would be the first target should war break out. Even the lukewarm efforts of state and local authorities to provide structures for civil defense added to the sense of impending violence.

Yet for all the apprehension experienced by Floridians, there was no sense of panic. Once the novelty of looking at the skies to observe planes passing overhead and once the sight of passing convoys of men and materiel became commonplace, citizens returned to their normal pursuits. On the Space Coast, the activities at Cape Canaveral was the focus of interest; in the Panhandle, citizens were concerned about what might be happening to the status of the many military bases in the area; in Tampa, MacDill AFB, which had been on the verge of closing, suddenly became a beehive of activity as squadron after squadron of aircraft took advantage of its multiple runways and hangars in preparation for any escalation in hostilities; in Orlando and Central Florida, daily activities continued at their pre-crisis level; and from Vero Beach to Fort Lauderdale, citizens noted the arrival of troops and aircraft with passing interest.

Southeast Florida, centered on Miami, was different. Cuban emigres, many newly arrived, were vocal in their support of the United States, while even more vocal in their dislike for Castro and the Soviet Union. Around the Miami area, army and air force personnel occupied World War II bases and isolated camps, equipped with nuclear-tipped missiles and bombs, and prepared for instant retaliation should the situation change from crisis to war. Miamians realized that they would be among the first casualties if warfare erupted. It was a sobering realization.

On October 22, President Kennedy delivered a speech to the nation that brought the crisis to a critical point. On October 23, he issued an ultimatum to Khrushchev and the Soviet Union that imposed an embargo on materiel going to Cuba and included a demand for the removal of Soviet missiles from that island nation. In the United Nations, diplomats watched the situation anxiously, uncertain whether the Soviets would comply and equally uncertain what the American response would be if Soviet compliance was not forthcoming. For several days, the world teetered on the edge of Armageddon. The stalemate was finally broken when a chartered freighter carrying supplies to Cuba complied with the embargo, followed rapidly by the dismantling of Soviet missile sites and the shipment of missiles back to their Russian bases. Within the space of two weeks, the world had been brought to the precipice of nuclear war, faced the possible horrors of "mutually assured destruction," and emerged from abyss through diplomacy and reason.

Despite the increasingly tense relationship between the Soviet Union and the United States, citizens in the Sunshine State remained focused on going about their normal activities. Churches opened their doors for those individuals who sought solace and assurances from their religious leaders, but little else changed. Civil governments took the time to leisurely consider implementing and funding a civil defense program, and a few public shelters were opened or designated for use.

Children, however, were the most impacted. "Duck and cover" drills, the collection of foodstuffs for emergency pantries, and the issuance of metal dog tags created a short-lived sense of danger, but the refusal of adults to engage in hysteria calmed them. Still in later years, these children, now adults, could remember the two weeks of the missile crisis in October 1962 quite vividly, although the cause for the crisis and its resolution remained vague.

The Sunshine State in October 1962 was a busy place, and although concerned about the possibility of a nuclear holocaust, its citizens were determined that they would simply persevere going about their normal activities. When presented with a golden opportunity to panic, they rejected fear and doubt. Their reactions to the crisis represent the best behavior from a resilient and brave people.

Selected Bibliography:
Florida and the Cuban Missile Crisis

Abel, Elie. *The Missile Crisis*. Philadelphia: J. P. Lippincott Company, 1966.

Beschloss, Michael R. *The Crisis Years: Kennedy and Khrushchev, 1960-1963*. New York: Edward Burlingame Books, 1991.

Bacon, Eve. *Orlando: A Centennial History*. Chuluota: Mickler House, 1977.

Blight, James G. and David A. Welch. "The Cuban Missile Crisis and Intelligence Performance." *Intelligence and National Security*. 2012.

Falcon, Manuel E. "Bay of Pigs and Cuban Missile Crisis: Presidential Decision Making and Its Effect on Military Employment During the Kennedy Administration." U. S. Army Command and General Staff College, Fort Leavenworth, Kansas, 1993.

Frankel, Max. *High Noon in the Cold War: Kennedy, Khrushchev, and the Cuban Missile Crisis*. New York: Ballantine Books, 2004.

Halberstam, David. *The Best and the Brightest*. New York: Random House, 1963.

Hansen, James H. "Soviet Deception in the Cuban Missile Crisis: Learning from the Past." https;//www.cia.gov/library/center-for-the-study-of-intelligence/csi-publications/csi-studies/...

Helms, Richard (With William Hood). *A Look Over My Shoulder: A Life in the Central Intelligence Agency.* New York: Ballantine Books, 2003.

Keithly, David. "Planes, Plans, Plots: How They Found the Missiles." *Journal of Strategic Studies.* 6(Fall 2013): 172-186.

Kennedy, Robert F. *Thirteen Days: A Memoir of the Cuban Missile Crisis.* New York: W. W. Norton, 1969.

Khrushchev, Nikita (with Introduction by Edward Crankshaw). *Khrushchev Remembers.* Boston: Little, Brown and Company, 1970.

McNamara, Robert. *In Retrospect: The Tragedy and Lessons of Viet Nam.* New York: Random House, 1995.

Martinez, Mel (with Ed Breslin). *A Sense of Belonging: From Castro's Cuba to the U. S. Senate, One Man's Pursuit of the American Dream.* New York: Crown Forum, 2008.

Patterson, Thomas G. "Fixation with Cuba: The Bay of Pigs, Missile Crisis, and Covert War Against Castro."

Sagan, Scott D. "SIOP-61: The Nuclear War Plan Briefing to President Kennedy." *International Security.* 12(Summer 1987): 22-51.

Wikenheiser, Frank Joseph. "The United States Military in the Cuban Missile Crisis." Master's Thesis, Florida State University, 1975.

Wittereid, Peter F. "A Strategy of Flexible Response." *Parameters.* (1972): 2-16.

Zegart, Amy. "The Cuban Missile Crisis as Intelligence Failure." *Policy Review.* (October-November 2012).

————•————

All essays in this volume used the local newspapers available in their areas. These include the *Orlando Sentinel*, the *Tallahassee Democrat, Pensacola News, Palm Beach Post, St. Petersburg Times, St. Petersburg Evening Independent, Tampa Tribune, Clearwater Sun, La Gaceta, Playground Daily News, Panama City News-Herald, Pensacola Journal, Cocoa Tribune, Melbourne Times, Titusville Star-Advocate, Florida Times-Union, Daytona Beach Morning Journal* and the *Santa Rosa Press-Gazette.*

CPSIA information can be obtained
at www.ICGtesting.com
Printed in the USA
FFOW02n2118261017
41574FF